DeLAURENTI
COOKBOOK

PAT McCARTHY & MATT SNYDER

JIM HENKENS
Photography

DOCUMENTARY MEDIA
Seattle

DELAURENTI COOKBOOK

DeLaurenti Food & Wine
1435 First Avenue
Seattle, WA 98101
800-873-6685
www.delaurenti.com

Published by Documentary Media LLC
3250 41st Avenue SW
Seattle, WA 98116
206-935-9292
books@docbooks.com
www.documentarymedia.com

First Edition
Printed in China

Authors: Pat McCarthy and Matt Snyder
Photographer: Jim Henkens
Designer: Jon Cannell
Editor: Judy Gouldthorpe
Executive Editor: Barry Provorse
Publisher: Petyr Beck

ISBN: 978-1-933245-28-7

Library of Congress Cataloging-in-Publication Data

McCarthy, Pat (Restaurant owner)
DeLaurenti Cookbook / Pat McCarthy and Matt Snyder ; Jim Henkens, Photography.
  pages cm
Includes index.
ISBN 978-1-933245-28-7 (alk. paper)
1. Cooking, Italian. 2. Cooking—Washington (State)—Seattle 3. DeLaurenti (Specialty food store)
4. Cookbooks. lcgft I. Snyder, Matt. II. Henkens, Jim. III. Title.
TX723.M394 2012
641.5945—dc23
            2012034128

CONTENTS

FOREWORD

Remember! Inspiration, tradition, memories, hospitality, passion—all centered around and on the TABLE, as it becomes the stage for the best play ever written.

Angelo Merlino played a key role in the genesis of Seattle's Italian culinary tradition. In 1903 or so, he opened an import food store on South Main Street, in lower downtown Seattle, in order to bring the foods that defined him from his home in Italy to his new community. He missed them: the flavors, the preparation, and the warmth they brought to his life and the lives of others from the old world. A warmth they remembered from their homelands.

This was his passion. He was driven by the understanding that many others like him felt the same way. There was nothing that resembled or tasted like that powerful cultural memory of the table—the hospitality it bred and the friendships that evolved around it.

Angelo wanted to recreate this memory by making available to people in the Northwest the cheeses, salumi and a myriad of other special products from his home country. His market thrived because of his foresight about location and products. In 1928 he moved into a building across the street from the U.S. Immigration Office, where all nationalities had to come to get work papers or enroll family members in the U.S. system. He also expanded his line of products to include Israel, Greece, Turkey, Spain, France, Germany, Corsica and Britain. Angelo was fulfilling his ambition to recreate the table of his culture, and that of others, right here in the Northwest.

The importance of this tradition, hospitality and passion cannot be overemphasized as we experience Pat McCarthy and Matt Snyder's *DeLaurenti Cookbook*. To keep alive the traditions and tastes of old, the wonderment of creating from the old into the new, the shaping of tomorrow with the fundamentals derived from "what was then"—that is, essentially, the history of DeLaurenti Food & Wine.

DeLaurentis have been in the Pike Place Market for some 11 decades, with family history that goes back to both the North of Italy—Florence, and Tuscany and Lombardy—and the South.

Pete DeLaurenti had worked for the old Seattle French Bakery. In 1946 he opened the first DeLaurenti market, called Pete's Italian Market (and later, DeLaurenti Italian Market). It flourished for some 30 years in that location, becoming a trademark of the Market, between the ramp and the specialty spice shop. Some of us still remember the bins of pasta, jars of olives, barrels and barrels of rice, the smell of cheeses. Many of these products are still available at DeLaurenti.

In the early seventies, Pete's son Lou DeLaurenti secured a space on the corner of First and Pike at street level (the old Bartell Drugs), and the new DeLaurenti opened in 1973. Eventually, as his father finally realized the value of the new space, the family closed the lower-level store. DeLaurenti became the cornerstone store and location at the Market, wildly popular in the retail trade for its diverse products from Europe and the Mediterranean.

Lou ran the business until the late '90s, when he decided to sell to Pat McCarthy, Matt Galvin and Pat McDonald. This decision was not taken lightly by any of them. It came out of many discussions, with all four of them struggling to understand and be clear about how DeLaurenti might continue on in the future and what it would take to make that happen. They did much of that thinking at Salumi when it opened—which I liked a lot because I could see how important it was to each of them. The potential new owners liked the modest beginnings of the history of DeLaurenti, and they understood the commitment it would take to move forth with the passion that was to be not just their jobs but also their lives. Thus was reborn the modern DeLaurenti: to serve people who create and recreate their own food traditions and love quality and artisan products. Today, Pat McCarthy and Matt Snyder present foods and ingredients traditional to the customers' cultures and memories, while also offering high-quality prepared food and drink with a spirit of hospitality as well as stories about it and the people who produce it.

They are unassuming and modest, but they constantly drive forward with their commitment to make available products with taste, aroma and texture that bring to life cultural memories and revive traditions. Harking back to a time when the first immigrants came from far and wide, but now part of a Northwest food culture of considerable sophistication, Pat and Matt have a great interest in preserving tradition and creating anew, through cooking, eating and sharing.

The table is the stage for carrying forth the traditions and cultures of life, and it is often the grandmother who bears responsibility for this task. As granddaughters of today become the grandmas of tomorrow, that role grows in importance. As do their love and the traditions they impart. Knowing and caring about where and how food is grown or made, its nutritional values—essentially everything about eating— inherently carries forward both a renewed spirit of the times and a rededication to the family table. Like grandma, DeLaurenti is carrying forward the memories and traditions of yesterday while creating new ones. This growing creative food spirit is and will be a part of Pat and Matt's future development of DeLaurenti: bringing sustainable products from all over the world to add richness to the wonders of the TABLE. A passionate mix that will be the great stage of tomorrow. What a play that is!

ARMANDINO BATALI

Founder, Salumi and Salumi Artisan Cured Meats

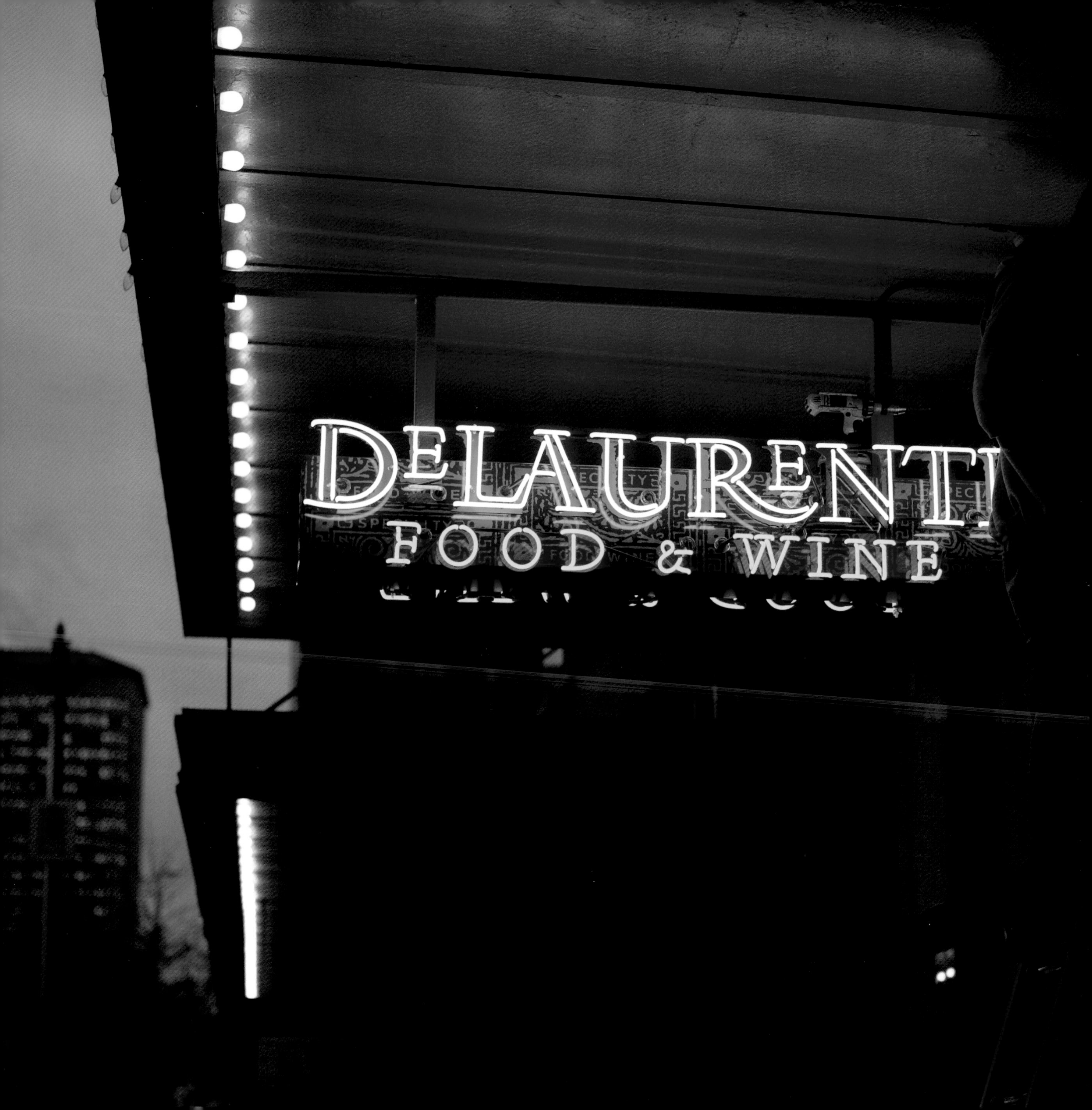
DELAURENT
FOOD & WINE

INTRODUCTION

Why write a book about DeLaurenti Food & Wine? Because it's a story worth telling and a landmark worth preserving. Very few cities have a store like DeLaurenti. Ours is a culinary archive and shop, preserved in order to cultivate and sustain the idea that food is important. Since 1946, DeLaurenti has honored the food traditions of generations of Seattleites by providing a source for the world's delicacies and ingredients. Food is not just a fuel; it's a life choice. DeLaurenti Food & Wine exists to serve those who value quality and tradition when considering their food choices.

What is your relationship with food? It's a question every job applicant is asked here at the store. If food is important to you, if food—the origin, sourcing, preparation, taste and sharing of it—matters to you, then food shapes your outlook on life; it's part of your soul. This experience of food is what defines DeLaurenti.

The store is known for many things: breadth and depth of products, service, quality ingredients, an amazing wine selection, and delicious café food and coffee. But what we are probably most renowned for is our deli. Indeed, our cheeses and cured meats are our most recognizable feature. Thousands of times per week, we provide knowledgeable and valuable service from our deli counter.

Our deli sets DeLaurenti apart from all the other cheese shops and grocery stores around. Nowhere else can you find 250 fresh cheeses and over 50 cured meats. And you certainly won't find as fresh a selection as we have. Take bread: we carry fresh bread from six local bakeries. You simply can't find that anywhere else. So, big deal, lots of choices. Well, exactly! We could carry just local foods or only French or Italian, or simply one prosciutto di Parma; many places do. But why not expose Seattle to the best the world has to offer? When you take the time to compare and appreciate them, you realize that every prosciutto di Parma has a unique flavor and lends itself to unique flavor opportunities. That's why we slice from up to seven different prosciutti at the counter.

What's local about that? The folks in Langhirano (a little commune near Parma, Italy) specialize in crafting this amazing food. Parma is local to them, for sure. We have the ability to bring their traditional cured ham to Seattle so our community can enjoy it the way Italians enjoy it. In fact, we bring in thousands of products—made in and appreciated in their own communities—to our store. We encourage you to enjoy local products, made by artisans and families around the world or a ferry ride away, here at our store. We understand "local" as a worthwhile value and mission and bring the products of other communities to our community.

A narrower definition of "local" might focus exclusively on foods from our region. There's nothing wrong with that. The Pacific Northwest has some of the most amazing foods and natural resources on the planet. But so does the Piedmont, the Loire Valley, the French Pyrenees, and Vermont. Our broader appreciation for "local" envelops the localness of the larger world. All of those places have local farms where caring people produce beautiful food, and we can get it to Seattle with a fair amount of effort. We say it's worth it. Bringing these foods to our community gives us a wealth of new ways to appreciate the foods we grow, raise, catch and craft right here on the shores of Puget Sound.

It starts with a visit to the deli. Every day we have folks step up to the cases hoping we can help them with an antipasti tray for a gathering of friends or family. It's one of our favorite questions. The truth is, we love what we sell and we eat what we sell. The best part for us? In a way, we get to be at your table or picnic or patio while you enjoy your meal with people you care about. We believe we can have a positive impact on people's daily lives not only by providing the delicious foods they share but also by providing a service experience worthy of their efforts to come to our shop.

DeLaurenti strives to be exactly what our customers and our city deserve: a culinary emporium inhabited by caring, devoted people who take their food—but not themselves—seriously.

Welcome to our store and our book about our store. It's filled with recipes we enjoy and use daily, some at the shop and some at home. You'll learn secrets (like our chocolate chip cookie recipe) and a few tricks (like how to burn lettuce and have it taste terrific). This isn't so much a cookbook as a snapshot of DeLaurenti Food & Wine— Seattle's culinary icon. A stake in the ground, so that folks who shop here 65 years from now will know what it was like way back when, and hopefully appreciate how much has stayed the same.

We are all stewards of this place, so thank you for helping us thrive.

See you at the store,

PAT McCARTHY & MATT SNYDER

THE KITCHEN

Plan Your Work, Work Your Plan – The French call it *mise en place*; others call it being organized. Whatever you call it, it's the right thing to do. Organized ingredients look nice, instill confidence, and make execution of any recipe easy.

Pans – There are two types: the ones you keep and the ones you replace. You need a good Dutch oven, a heavy-bottomed pasta pot with a strainer, a trusty sauté pan, two reliable skillets—one nonstick—and a broad saucepan with high sides. Add to this list as your budget dictates. No shame in working with what you have in the meantime.

Salt – Want things to taste good? Use enough. Operative word: *enough*. Be conservative early, taste often, and leave room to finish. If your dish is lacking something, it's probably salt.

Your Home Is Not a Restaurant – Leave the foam, blast freezers and food science to the pros. Trade these things in for seasonal ingredients and simple preparations. You will get better results and be equally as revered by your friends and family.

Sharp Knives – If you are going to cut yourself, you can do so with a sharp knife or a dull one. There is greater honor in doing so with a sharp blade. Plus, you will have the advantage of cutting tomatoes and onions, not crushing them.

A Three-Liter Tin of Olive Oil, an Empty Wine Bottle and a Pouring Spout – If there are more than two people in your family and you don't buy olive oil in a three-liter tin, there is something wrong. The "it will go bad" argument can be solved by using it. Keep the tin in the cupboard, choose a wine bottle that felt good in your hand while you were drinking it, fill it up with oil, put a pouring spout in it, and keep that on your counter. Ample oil at the ready, and nothing spoiled.

No Substitutions, Please – Margarine, sweeteners in colorful packages, or products whose list of ingredients belongs in a science journal should be avoided.

Microplane – For shaving, grating and zesting. A must. It should not look like the standup grater, which should be reserved for producing large mounds of grated Cheddar.

Pin-Boning Tool – Some say you shouldn't buy single-use kitchen tools. This is an exception. Stop borrowing your wife's tweezers— she's tired of having them smell like fish. And stop using the needle-nose pliers that you used on the fence. They are rusty and rip up the flesh of the 50-dollar piece of king salmon you just bought.

Charcoal Whenever Possible – There is no debate on what makes food taste better. The question is whether the gain is greater than the effort invested. If the answer is yes, keep doing it. If the answer is no, say it with conviction, and keep some wood chips around to use with your gas grill. If you don't have a grill, get a good grill pan.

Peppermill – A good one is not cheap, but a good one is essential. It doesn't have to be over 12 inches tall, but it does have to be effective.

Mandoline – You won't use this every day, but when you need it, it's the only tool that will do the job.

In a Bowl, Not a Shaker – Keep your kosher salt in your favorite bowl on the counter. Feel the texture of the grains in your fingers as you properly season all of your sauces, meats and soups. You literally have the power at your fingertips: the power to make things taste good.

Fish Spatula – This is the only tool to effectively lift and flip a delicate piece of fish out of your favorite sauté pan. It has to be stiff, with a thin beveled edge and a solid handle.

Your Hands – The best tools in the kitchen. Make sure they are clean, and don't be afraid to use them.

Tongs – An extension of your hands. Two pairs minimum. Basic is good. Too short, you burn your hand. Too long, they are cumbersome and you'll lack control.

MEAT, CHEESE & ANTIPASTI

Parmigiano-Reggiano – This doesn't come in a green can, and doesn't come wrapped in plastic. Buy it from a place that sells a lot of it, and use it unashamedly—just not on your fish.

Prosciutto – When sliced perfectly, it is paper-thin, peels off in one piece, and almost melts in your mouth.

Pecorino Romano – A staple like Parmigiano-Reggiano. Your only choice for Bucatini all'Amatriciana.

The Cheese on Your Counter – Don't be afraid to leave it there before enjoying it. If it starts to smell, cover it, but don't put it back in the fridge. Room temperature is a great ally.

Raw Milk – It's good. The government can't protect you from everything, including flavor and tradition. You ingest more chemicals and assume more risk crossing the street in downtown Seattle.

Choosing Your Cheese – First, ask. There is always something in our case that is perfect now, or will soon be gone. Second, keep the numbers down; too many things on the plate are confusing. Last, mix it up: the milk types, the textures or places of origin.

Fresh Mozzarella – The most versatile cheese in the case. At home on a refined cheese plate and on a pizza.

When in Doubt – Call *800.873.6685*.

CHARCUTERIE

A few of our favorites.

CURED & COOKED

Bresaola
Air-cured beef loin from the Lombardy region in northern Italy. Great sliced paper thin on its own or as a substitute for beef carpaccio. Drizzle with extra-virgin olive oil, a squeeze of lemon and black pepper. Or serve it with fresh arugula, shaved Parmigiano-Reggiano and a drizzle of truffle oil.

Carnegie Corned Beef
The classic Carnegie Deli corned beef, made the same way since 1937 in New York City.

Carnegie Pastrami
The classic Carnegie Deli pastrami, made the same way since 1937 in New York City.

Fabrique Délices Saucisson à l'Ail
Select pork seasoned with fresh and roasted garlic. Cut on the thicker side and enjoy with a traditional French baguette.

German Black Forest Ham
Made exclusively in Germany's Black Forest region. Salted and seasoned by hand. Air dried and then gently smoked over fir wood to give it its pronounced smoky character. Enjoy sliced paper thin with dark, hearty bread and fruit.

Italian Mortadella with Pistachios
The origin of all bologna. Delicate and tender. Perfect sliced paper thin on a crusty loaf with extra-virgin olive oil or fantastic sliced thick, grilled and drizzled with balsamic vinegar.

Italian Porchetta
Pork tenderloin wrapped in bacon—seasoned, rolled, tied and roasted. At home on your antipasti platter or on a panini with grilled fennel and Pecorino Romano.

Jambon
Classic French-style cooked ham—delicious and sweet. Perfect on a baguette with Comté, Dijon mustard and cornichons.

Salumi Hot Coppa
Handmade dry-cured pork shoulder with red chiles in the traditional style of Emilia-Romagna. Slice it paper thin and it will melt in your mouth. Great on pizza and sandwiches or as part of an antipasto.

Tuscan Rosemary Ham
Seasoned with rosemary, salt and fresh pepper and roasted to perfection. Great for sandwiches, eggs or pizza. Also fantastic sliced thick and grilled on the barbecue with peppers and onions.

Vande Rose Farms Ham
Artisanally crafted from 100% Iowa Duroc hormone-free pigs. Applewood smoked and cured with a touch of brown sugar. Great for everything from sandwiches to split pea soup.

The Pigs

The secret of Parma ham begins with a careful and accurate selection of the pigs. Parma pigs must be specially bred Large White, Landrace and Duroc breeds, born and raised in 11 regions of central-northern Italy. Their diet is a regulated blend of grains, cereals and whey from Parmigiano-Reggiano cheese production, ensuring a heavy pig with a moderate daily growth in an excellent state of health. The pigs are at least nine months old and must weigh a minimum of 140 kilograms at the time of slaughter.

The Process

The hams are made from the rear haunches of the pigs with four essential ingredients: Italian pigs, salt, air and time. Additives such as sugar, spices, smoke, water and nitrites are prohibited. Making Prosciutto di Parma is a long and painstaking process. The curing is controlled carefully so that the ham absorbs only enough salt to preserve it. By the end, a trimmed ham will have shrunk more than 25% due to moisture loss, helping to concentrate the flavor. The meat becomes tender, and the distinctive aroma and flavor of Prosciutto di Parma emerge.

Trimming: A portion of skin and fat are removed to give the ham its typical drumstick shape.

Salting: A highly trained *maestro salatore*, or salt master, rubs sea salt into the meat, which is then refrigerated at 80% humidity for about a week. Residual salt is removed and the ham gets a second thin coating of salt, which is left on for another 15 to 18 days depending on weight. By making daily adjustments in temperature and humidity, the *maestro* ensures that the legs absorb just enough salt to cure them.

Resting: The hams hang for 70 days in refrigerated, humidity-controlled rooms, at 65% humidity. The meat darkens but will return to its original rosy color in the final days of curing.

Washing and Drying: The hams are washed with warm water and brushed to remove excess salt, then hung in drying rooms.

Initial Curing: The hams are hung on frames in well-ventilated rooms with large windows that are opened when the outside temperature and humidity are favorable. Connoisseurs believe that this period, when the hams are bathed in aromatic breezes, is critical to the development of their distinctive flavor. By the end of this phase, which lasts about three months, the exposed surface of the meat has dried and hardened.

Greasing: The exposed surfaces of the hams are softened with a paste of minced lard and salt.

Final Curing: The hams are moved to dark, cellarlike rooms and hang on racks until the curing is completed. The hams are cured for at least a year, and some for as long as 30 months.

PROSCIUTTO & SERRANO

Jamón Ibérico
One of the world's great delicacies. The *pata negra*, or black hoof, is made only from black Iberian hogs. These hams are categorized according to their diet. Jamón Ibérico de Bellota, the most prized, feeds exclusively on acorns. The next grade, Jamón Ibérico de Recebo, feeds on a combination of grains and acorns. The last, Jamón Ibérico de Cebo, feeds on grains alone. All of the grades are prized for their exceptionally smooth texture and rich taste. To fully appreciate Jamón Ibérico, it should be enjoyed simply.

Prosciutto di Parma - Leporati
See sidebar.

Prosciutto di Parma - Leporati Black Label
Aged two years, giving it a more concentrated flavor than its 18-month counterpart.

Prosciutto di Parma - Pio Tosini
Aged a minimum of 500 days by one of the best producers in Parma. Incomparably sweet and delicate.

San Daniele Prosciutto
From the region of Friuli-Venezia Giulia, in northeast Italy. The sweet and complex character of Prosciutto di San Daniele is the result of fresh breezes from the Dolomites mingling with the humid winds from the nearby Adriatic Sea.

Serrano Ham
Traditional and ubiquitous Spanish ham made from pigs born and raised in the Salamanca region of western Spain. Salted and aged for over a year in clean mountain air. Intensely flavorful and a touch firmer than Prosciutto di Parma. Slice it paper thin and enjoy it with your favorite Spanish cheese, olives and crusty bread.

Speck
Mildly smoked and air-cured ham from South Tyrol, Italy's northern-most province. Made from the pig's rear thigh, boned and seasoned with salt, pepper, juniper and a touch of sugar. Traditionally sliced thick and enjoyed with hearty bread. It is also lovely sliced paper thin as an antipasto.

SALAME & CHORIZO

Alps Cacciatorini
Handmade hunter's salame, rich and flavorful. Perfect for a picnic.

Alps Sopressata - Hot or Sweet
Artisan, handmade sopressata from Astoria in Queens, New York. Hot and sweet. Great on pizza or with antipasti.

Creminelli Barolo
This handmade salame has a robust flavor that comes from a generous amount of Barolo red wine that is added to Creminelli's traditional salame recipe. Great lingering finish.

Creminelli Tartufo
Handmade salame with black summer truffles. Lightly seasoned to allow the delicate earthy aroma and flavor of truffles to emerge.

Creminelli Whiskey
Creminelli artisan salame and High West Distillery's Son of Bourye come together for a uniquely delicious take on salame. Redolent of whiskey and richly flavored.

Creminelli Wild Boar
Wild Boar salame is a mixture of field-harvested Texas wild boar and all-natural pork belly, seasoned with cloves and juniper berries for a robust yet sweet flavor.

Fra'Mani Salame Gentile
A traditional, handmade salame whose origins date back to the 18th century in Parma, Italy. Coarsely ground and encased in *budello gentile*, from which it takes its name and shape. Rich and buttery.

Fra'Mani Salame Nostrano
"Nostrano" means "our own." Handmade, coarse-ground salame that is mild and sweet. Great with melon and figs.

Fra'Mani Sopressata
Modeled after sopressa Vincentina from the Vincenza province in northeastern Italy. Coarsely chopped. Hints of clove and garlic. Moist and full flavored.

Olympic Provisions Loukanika
Handmade Greek salame flavored with equal parts garlic and cumin, and a touch of orange zest.

Olympic Provisions Saucisson d'Alsace
Handmade Alsatian pub salame flavored with clove, nutmeg, allspice and cinnamon.

Olympic Provisions Saucisson Sec
Handmade traditional French salame flavored with garlic and black pepper.

Palacios Spanish Chorizo
The first authentic Spanish chorizo available in the U.S. Fully cured and ready to eat. Flavored with hot or mild *pimentón*. Pair with Spanish sheep's milk cheeses and Marcona almonds.

Rosette de Lyon
Artisan, handmade, French-style salame, made from 100% Berkshire pork. Coarse grind, soft in texture and very buttery.

Salumi Finocchiona
A Salumi and DeLaurenti favorite. Made with an abundance of black pepper, cracked fennel seed and a touch of curry.

Salumi Hot Sopressata
Spicy salame with garlic, a vibrant red color and warm finish.

Salumi Mole
Salumi's most unusual creation, and perhaps its most popular. Flavored with chocolate, cinnamon, and ancho and chipotle peppers.

Salumi Oregano
Herbacious and flavorful. Prepared with fragrant oregano from Bainbridge Island.

Salumi Rosmarino
Developed and made especially for DeLaurenti. Our house salame, made with fresh rosemary from Bainbridge Island, black pepper and garlic.

Salumi Salami
Salumi's first salame. Mildly seasoned with a touch of ginger.

Silva Spanish-Style Chorizo
Seasoned with bay leaf, oregano, paprika and garlic. Great in paella, on the grill or with your eggs.

SAUSAGE, BACON & PANCETTA

Cascioppo Brothers Sausage
Made by hand in Ballard and delivered daily for over 30 years. The best in the city.

Leoncini Pancetta
Fully cooked slab pancetta from Lazise in northern Italy. Slow cooked in dry-air ovens and naturally smoked.

Molinari Pancetta
Semi-cured, seasoned, rolled pork belly—Italian bacon. Makes simple pastas amazing. Great for meat sauces and roasted vegetables.

Nueske's Applewood Smoked Bacon
Made in Wisconsin from a family recipe since 1933. Patiently smoked over applewood embers for more than 24 hours. Lean but packed with flavor. Cut to order.

Salumi Guanciale
Cured and seasoned pork jowl, used like bacon or pancetta. An indispensable ingredient in your pasta carbonara. Locally made in Seattle by Armandino Batali.

Salumi Pancetta
High-quality pork belly, rolled, semi-cured and spiced with black pepper. Handmade in Seattle by Salumi.

CHEESE

A few of our favorites.

BLUE

Beenleigh Blue
Pasteurized sheep's milk blue made by Ben Harris and Robin Congdon in Devon, England. Firm and a bit crumbly. All at once tangy, pleasantly salty, sweet and nutty.

Bleu de Brebis
Raw alpine sheep's milk blue from the Basque region of the Pyrenees. Firm and slightly crumbly paste. Dense and mild, with hints of grass and fruit.

Bleu du Bocage
A raw goat's milk blue from the Loire Valley in France. Dense, concentrated and bright. Salty, grassy, sweet and spicy.

Fourme d'Ambert
One of France's oldest cheeses, with production dating back to Roman times. Made from pasteurized cow's milk in the Auvergne. Velvety and sweet, with a touch of earth.

Gorgonzola Dolce
Produced since 1876 by Guffanti in the Piedmont region of northern Italy. Creamy, sweet, silky and spreadable. Full flavored but mild.

Gorgonzola Piccante
Produced since 1876 by Guffanti in the Piedmont region of northern Italy. Semi-firm, densely creamy paste with widespread blueing. Piquant, robust and assertive.

Harbourne Blue
One of only a handful of goat's milk blues made in England. Created by Robin Congdon and produced in the Sharpham area of Devon. Spicy and assertive.

Maytag Blue
An Iowa original since 1941. Bright, tangy, cakey blue made from the milk of Maytag Dairy's prize-winning herd of Holstein cattle.

Point Reyes Original Blue
Raw milk blue from northern California. Solid and flaky in texture, bright and tangy with dark blue/green vein.

Roquefort
The King of French Blues. Made with 100% raw sheep's milk and aged in the caves of Roquefort-sur-Soulzon in southern France. Assertive, salty, sweet, earthy and piquant.

Stilton
The King of English Blues. The last hand-ladled Stilton in the world, from Colston Bassett. Rich, buttery and dense, with a minerally tang. Strong and full without being overpowering.

Valdeón
Cow's and goat's milk blue from Castilla y León in Spain. Wrapped in sycamore leaves, which provide a distinctive appearance and complex flavor. Hearty and densely veined, with a nice balance of salt and spice.

CHEDDAR/BRITISH ISLES

Appleby's Cheshire
Made by Garry Gray and the Appleby family in Shropshire, England. Moistly flaky raw cow's milk cheese with a crumbly texture and a savory, lactic tang.

Appleby's Double Gloucester
Raw cow's milk cheese made by Garry Gray and the Appleby family in Shropshire, England. Smooth and creamy texture. Slightly tangy with a minerally bite.

Ardrahan
The flavor is more subtle than the aroma would suggest. Washed rind, earthy and pungent. Rich, soft and sticky paste with pungent, savory and smoky flavors.

Cabot Clothbound Cheddar
Aged for a minimum of 10 months in the cellars at Jasper Hill Farm, in Vermont. Reminiscent of a classic English Cheddar, it is all at once sweet, savory, nutty and tangy.

Hawes Wensleydale
Traditional cow's milk cheese made by the Hawes Creamery in North Yorkshire, England. Finely textured, flaky and moist. Gentle and approachable, with a subtle tart freshness.

Isle of Mull Cheddar

Raw cow's milk Cheddar made by Chris and Jeff Reade, from the Isle of Mull, near Tobermory in Scotland. Moist and soft in texture with a barnyard fruitiness.

Keen's Cheddar

Raw cow's milk Cheddar made by the Keen family at Moorhayes Farm near Wincanton, Somerset. Smooth and firm in texture, rich and nutty, with a pleasant tangy finish.

Kirkham's Lancashire

Raw cow's milk cheese made by Graham Kirkham at Lower Beesley Farm near Goosnargh, Lancashire. Lemony, reminiscent of tangy yogurt. Moist in texture, rich and creamy with a classic butter crumble.

Montgomery's Cheddar

Rich, sweet, fruity and nutty. Drier than most Cheddars with a grainy and crystallized crunch as it ages.

Quebec Cheddar

Cow's milk Cheddar aged over four years. Dry and crumbly with a sharp and tangy flavor.

COW'S MILK

Camembert

Traditional small-production Camembert from the Normandy region in France, ripened by French *affineur* Hervé Mons. The paste is deeply golden, supple and yielding. Earthy and buttery, with pleasant aromas of mushrooms and truffles.

Cantal

Made in the Auvergne, Cantal is one of France's most traditional large-format cow's milk cheeses. Semi-firm, moist and slightly crumbly with a natural rind mottled with brown-, gray- and rust-colored molds. Mild and accessible with hints of butter, fresh milk, nuts, citrus and caramel.

Coolea

Irish cow's milk cheese crafted from an old Dutch Gouda recipe by Dick Willems near the small village of Coolea. Covered in a thick, solid wax rind, it is smooth and closely textured. Rich and sweet with notes of hazelnuts, butterscotch and honey.

Dinah's Cheese

A luscious, soft, buttery Camembert-style cheese made by Kurt Timmermeister at Kurtwood Farms on Vashon Island. Bloomy rind, with an ivory paste and a rich satiny texture.

Epoisses

Cow's milk cheese from Burgundy that is washed in marc. Pungent and barnyardy in aroma, it is full flavored, sweet, milky and slightly salty. Meltingly soft and unctuous.

Fromage de Meaux

Made in the Ile-de-France region of northern France—the pasteurized version of Brie de Meaux. White, velvety rind with a straw-colored paste. Slightly sweet and smoky with aromas of mushrooms and truffles. Rich, buttery and smooth with a pleasant hint of bitterness.

Mimolette Vieille

Produced in the town of Lille, in the Pas-de-Calais region of northern France. Raw cow's milk cheese with a rustic, pitted rind and a unique spherical shape resembling a cantaloupe. The paste is dense, hard and smooth, with a vibrant orange color. Notes of caramel, butterscotch and toasted nuts.

Morbier

Raw cow's milk cheese produced in the village of Morez in the Jura Mountains of France. Semi-soft, supple and springy in texture, with small eyes and a distinctive layer of ash running through the center. The straw-yellow paste is much milder in flavor than the pungent washed rind. Fruity, barnyardy and grassy.

Pleasant Ridge Reserve

Award-winning raw cow's milk cheese from Uplands Cheese in southern Wisconsin. Washed orange-brown rind, with a texture that is firm but smooth. The caramel-golden paste is rich, deep and smooth with hints of caramel, salt, grass and flora.

Raclette

One of the world's great melting cheeses, and one of the most beloved dishes in the French and Swiss Alps. Robust flavor with a silken texture and perfect melting characteristics. Pair with cold cuts, steamed yellow potatoes, cornichons, pickled onions and wine from the Savoie.

Winnimere

Developed by Mateo Kehler at Jasper Hill Farm. Made from raw cow's milk, wrapped in cambium cut from spruce trees, and washed in beer from Hill Farmstead Brewery. Has remarkable variation from batch to batch—sometimes smoky, sometimes fruity, sometimes mustardy, sometimes meaty. Spoonably soft and molten.

GOUDA, FRENCH/SWISS ALPINE

Beaufort

A raw cow's milk cheese made in the Haute-Savoie region of France dating back to Roman times. Dense and slightly granular in texture. Pungent and pleasantly barnyardy, with flavors of fresh grass, fruit and butter.

Challerhocker

Means "sitting in the cellar." Washed in wine and spices and aged for a minimum of 10 months. Deep in flavor, firm yet creamy. Notes of roasted nuts and butterscotch with a touch of fruit.

Comté

Chosen and imported by the Essex St. Cheese Company by flavor profile, not by age and price. Aromas of hazelnuts, onions and strawberries mix with grass and earth. Dense, creamy, fruity and herbaceous.

Emmentaler AOC

AOC Swiss raw cow's milk cheese from the Emmental Valley in the canton of Berne, produced since the 13th century. In its youth it is semi-hard, mild and nutty, becoming more aromatic and intense as it ages. Known for its characteristically cherry-sized holes that occur during the fermentation process.

Gruyère 1655

Named for Gruyère's year of origin. This traditional alpine cheese is made by an exclusive trio of very small farms in the Swiss Alps. Earthy, nutty and assertive, with a dense texture and a lively crunch.

L'Amuse Gouda

Made at the Cono cheesemaking plant in Northern Holland. All the wheels are hand-selected and matured for two years. The paste color is deep amber with well-distributed protein crystals. An aroma of roasted hazelnuts and caramel complements the velvety texture. Nutty and salty with a long finish of burnt caramel.

Maxx 365

From the Thurgau region in northeast Switzerland, this cheese is the aged version of Scharfe Maxx. Made from raw whole cow's milk with a touch of cream added. Firm in texture, but uncommonly rich and creamy. Fruity, nutty and grassy.

Prima Donna

Dutch cow's milk aged for 14 to 16 months. Semi-soft with a subtle crystalline texture. Sweet and nutty with a caramel finish.

ITALIAN COW & SHEEP

Burrata

Traditionally from Puglia in southern Italy, this is the freshest of cow's milk cheeses. Milky, sweet, fresh mozzarella on the outside with an interior of molten ribbons of curd and cream.

Fontina Val d'Aosta

Semi-firm, washed-rind cheese from northwest Italy with a mildly pungent aroma. Rich and nutty with subtle flavors of fruit and grass. One of the world's great melting cheeses, and the centerpiece of the Piedmont's famous fondutta, a fondue-like blend of Fontina Val d'Aosta, cream, eggs and shaved white truffles.

La Tur

A dense, creamy blend of cow's, goat's and sheep's milk from the Piedmont in northern Italy. Runny and molten on the outside, moist and cakey on the inside. Rich and sweet, with a subtle tang.

Moliterno al Tartufo

Produced on the island of Sardinia off the coast of Italy. Aged raw sheep's milk cheese that has been injected with thick veins of black truffle. Dark ivory paste interspersed with solid lines of black truffle. Intense truffle flavor with a pleasantly crumbly texture.

Mozzarella di Bufala

Fresh mozzarella made from water buffalo's milk, originally from the Campania region in southern Italy. The rich milk curd is spun into a pillowy fresh mozzarella. Buttery, grassy and tangy.

Parmigiano-Reggiano

The king of Italian cheeses. Made from raw cow's milk only in the areas near Parma, Reggio Emilia, Modena, Bologna and Mantova. Aged a minimum of 12 months, Consorzio tested. Use on almost everything except your fish.

Parmigiano-Reggiano Vacche Rosse

Made exclusively from the raw milk of the Reggiana breed of cow, known for its beautiful red coat (vacche rosa). This cheese tastes like the Parmigiano-Reggiano of days gone by. Higher in butterfat and natural proteins, its more fruity, nutty and grassy flavor surpasses that of traditional Parmigiano-Reggiano. Reserve for special dishes, or eating on its own laced with aged balsamic vinegar.

Pecorino Ginepro

Semi-hard sheep's milk cheese from Emilia-Romagna, washed in balsamic vinegar and steeped in juniper. Full-flavored with a hint of sweetness, and very subtle juniper.

Pecorino di Manciano

Aged sheep's milk cheese from Tuscany. Firm, dry, nutty and sweet. Great as a table cheese or for grating.

Pecorino Romano

The last Pecorino Romano still produced exclusively in the village of Nepi outside Rome. Sharp and salty, it is not as firm as its Sardinian counterparts. Perfect for shaving and grating, or paired with honey and pears for dessert.

Piave Vecchio

Made with pasteurized cow's milk in the Veneto, in northern Italy. Nutty, concentrated and sweet. Lightly crystallized, with tropical aromas. Perfect for shaving or as a table cheese.

Provolone Valpadana

Consorzio certified and produced in the town of Cremona in northern Italy. Made from raw cow's milk and aged for over eight months. Intensely piquant, strong, nutty, fruity and just salty enough.

Taleggio

Semi-soft, washed-rind cow's milk cheese named after the Taleggio Valley in Lombardy. One of the world's oldest soft cheeses. Pungent in aroma, yet milder in flavor. Yeasty, mushroomy, fruity and tangy. Moist and spreadable when perfect.

SHEEP & GOAT TOMME

Abbaye de Belloc

Sheep's milk cheese from the Pyrenees made in the traditional manner by Benedictine monks at the abbey of Notre-Dame de Belloc. Fine, dense and smooth in texture. Sweet and mild with hints of brown butter, nuts and caramel.

Berkswell

Raw sheep's milk cheese made at Ram Hall near Berkswell, England. Rich, sweet, tropical and nutty. Bears the distinctive imprint of being pressed by hand in a colander, giving the cheese its unique rustic rind and flying-saucer-like shape. Firm and dense in texture and slightly granular, with an interior paste the color of pale butter.

Brebis de Wavreumont

Organic raw sheep's milk cheese from Belgium. Semi-hard with an ivory paste and a creamy, lush mouthfeel. Made in the Belgian monastic tradition, it is mild with a hint of sweetness.

Caprotto

Produced and aged by the Madaio family in the Campania region in southern Italy. A firm, unpasteurized goat's milk cheese with an ivory- to amber-colored paste, depending on how long it's aged. Intense aromas of hazelnuts and flowers with a delicate earthen flavor.

Dylan

Made by Yarmuth Farms in Darrington, Washington. Farmhouse-style table cheese made from raw goat's milk and aged over 60 days. Fresh and buttery with a hint of lemon.

Gabietou

Washed-rind cheese made from cow's and sheep's milk. Semi-soft, smooth and supple with a pale, straw-colored paste and occasional holes or "eyes." The rind is thin, with a golden-orange color. The aroma is slightly pungent, but not overwhelming. Dense, rich and creamy, with notes of fruit and earth.

Aged Manchego

Aged raw sheep's milk cheese from the La Mancha region, just south of Madrid. Intense and nutty, with a lovely sweetness. Pairs well with Marcona almonds, quince paste and cured chorizo.

Paški Šir

Firm and distinctive sheep's milk cheese from the Croatian island of Pag. Firm and golden with pleasant crystallization. Nutty with a hint of sweetness.

Tête de Moine

Cow's milk cheese produced by nine village dairies in the Bernese Jura Mountains in Switzerland. Tête de Moine, meaning "monk's head," has a firm, straw-colored paste with a spicy, fruity aroma. Often shaved using a special cutter called a girolle, creating beautiful, delicate flowers of cheese.

Tin Willow Tomme

Tomme made with sheep's milk from the Tin Willow Farm in Lexington, Oregon, by Black Sheep Creamery in Washington. Semi-firm with flavors of grass, sage and roasted nuts.

SOFT RIPENED & FRESH

Adelle

Soft-ripened, bloomy pasteurized blend of cow's and sheep's milk cheese from Ancient Heritage Dairy in Madras, Oregon. Light, fluffy, creamy and smooth, with a buttery hint of citrus.

Bosina

A creamy blend of cow's and sheep's milk from the Langhe region in northern Italy. Shaped like a small, square pillow. It has an ivory paste that is luxurious and silky—mild, sweet and milky.

Calabro Fresh Ricotta

Award-winning ricotta from the Calabro company in Connecticut. Light, fluffy and creamy, with a milky sweetness.

Fresh Chevre - Rollingstone

The signature farmstead cheese from Rollingstone Chevre in Parma, Idaho. Rich, ultra-creamy, bright and tangy.

Couronne de Touraine

Also known as Couronne Lochoise. Named for its unique donut-like shape: *couronne*, meaning crown. Soft ripened, ash-covered goat cheese from the Loire, produced by Rodolphe Le Meunier. Fondue-like just under the rind, firm but not chalky in the center. Tangy and minerally, with notes of fresh hay.

DeLaurenti Fresh Mozzarella

"Fior di Latte," the flower of the milk. Traditional fresh mozzarella made fresh every morning at the shop. Soft, sweet and milky.

Le Lingot du Quercy

Handmade goat cheese from a small collection of farms in Quercy, France. Distinctively shaped like a gold ingot. Molten and creamy just under the naturally forming rind, cakey and dense in the middle. Rich and slightly grassy, with a tangy finish.

Pico

French goat's milk cheese that resembles a petite Camembert. Richly earthy, smooth and creamy, surrounded by a thin, delicate rind.

Pierre Robert

Made from pasteurized cow's milk in the Ile-de-France region of France. Decadent triple crème that is extremely rich and buttery, yet relatively mild in flavor.

St. Marcellin

Soft-ripened disk of sweet cow's milk cheese presented in a small decorative crock. Mushroomy, truffly and slightly earthy, growing more molten and assertive as it ages. Gently heat St. Marcellin in the oven and serve with a fresh baguette.

FRESH MOZZARELLA

Buying and eating fresh mozzarella is good. Making and eating fresh mozzarella is better. This process happens seven days a week at DeLaurenti. Customers make a special trip to the store to buy mozzarella that is so fresh and tender, the brine is still warm. Although the process appears a bit daunting, it is actually quite simple. All that is required is curd, salt, water and practice. Soon

you will be enjoying your creation on a crusty loaf of bread, with a perfect heirloom tomato, or on your favorite pizza. If you need curd and a few tips to get started, just come to DeLaurenti. If after reading this, you are still hesitant to try, don't worry—we are happy to keep making it for you.

INGREDIENTS

1 gallon water

1 cup kosher salt, plus more
    for cooling water

3 pounds cheese curd

Pour the water into a large pot and add the salt. Heat over medium-high until the water reaches 178°F. Reduce the heat to low and maintain the temperature, monitoring frequently. Note: Maintaining the correct water temperature is essential in achieving the right consistency. If the water is too hot, the finished cheese will flatten out. If it is too cold, it will not come together properly.

Fill a large 3- to 4-inch-deep baking dish half full of cool tap water. Add 1 tablespoon salt per ½ gallon of water.

Place the curd on a clean cutting board and dice into ¼-inch cubes. Transfer to a large bowl and set aside.

Add a few large handfuls of curd to a separate bowl. Using a pitcher or large ladle, transfer enough heated salt water to cover the curd in the bowl.

Gently stir the curd, making sure that the cubes are not bound together. This will encourage even heating. Let it bathe for a few minutes, until it has the consistency of soft putty. The curd should start coming together as a single piece.

Drain the water from the bowl and submerge the curd in a second bath of heated salt water. With gentle pressure, run a rubber spatula over the curd, smoothing it out until it is one smooth mass. Using your hands (it may be a bit warm), turn the ball of curd over on itself until all the curd has the same soft, smooth consistency. Do not overwork the curd.

Pull off a piece of curd the size of a billiard ball and begin working it into shape. Cup both hands and hold the curd with palms facing up.

Gently move the thumbs and heel of the hand down over the top while rotating it to create a smooth surface. At the same time, gently push up with the other fingers, almost as if shaping a mushroom cap.

Begin to seal the under portion by gently pinching the curd together with one hand and pushing it up through the other hand, which is held in the shape of a C. Gently narrow the passage as the ball is pushed through the collar of the C until it rests on top of the other hand.

Holding the finished cheese from the bottom, carefully place it in the cool water. Let the finished mozzarella rest for 5 to 10 minutes so it will firm up and hold its shape. Repeat the process with the remaining curd.

Enjoy immediately, or refrigerate and use within 24 to 48 hours.

To drink: Prosecco, Vermentino, Falanghina

BURRATA

When you've mastered mozzarella making, you may want another challenge worth undertaking. Burrata is such a challenge. We decided to start making it ourselves when importing burrata from Italy became prohibitively expensive. We experimented and eventually created our own version of this unique cheese. It's no wonder that the most heavily attended and fascinating demonstrations during the Seattle Cheese Festival, held in May each year at the Pike Place Market, featured burrata making. Try this recipe and be sure to have plenty of bread and friends around as soon as it's ready.

INGREDIENTS

1 gallon water

1 cup kosher salt

3 pounds cheese curd

1 quart heavy cream

1 large, wide stainless steel bowl

1 small bowl, 4 inches in diameter at the lip

6 6-inch squares of cheesecloth

6 6-inch lengths of kitchen twine

6 plastic sandwich bags

Pour the water into a large pot and add the salt. Heat over medium-high until the water reaches 178°F. Reduce the heat to low and maintain the temperature, monitoring frequently. Note: Maintaining the correct water temperature is essential in achieving the right consistency. If the water is too hot, the finished cheese will flatten. If it is too cold, it will not come together properly.

Fill a 3- to 4-inch-deep baking dish half full of room-temperature tap water.

Place the curd on a clean cutting board and dice into ¼-inch cubes. Transfer to a large bowl and set aside.

First, prepare the filling: In a large saucepan over medium heat, gently simmer the cream until reduced by half, approximately 20 minutes. Stir frequently and be careful not to scald the cream. When finished, the cream should coat the back of a wooden spoon. Remove from the heat and transfer to a shallow bowl to cool for 5 to 10 minutes.

Place 2 cups of diced curd in the large stainless steel bowl. Using a small pitcher or ladle, cover the curd with hot salt water until

completely submerged, and stir gently. When the curd has softened to a putty-like texture and begun to come together (1 to 2 minutes), drain in a colander and then return to the bowl and submerge the curd in a second bath until it is fully melted into one smooth mass (1 to 2 minutes).

Remove the curd from the water and gently form into a ball. On a clean cutting board, push the curd out into a pancake shape approximately ¼ inch thick, then mince as finely as possible. Add the minced curd to the cooled reduced cream and stir. When finished, the filling should resemble creamy cottage cheese. Set aside.

Line the interior of the 4-inch bowl with one of the pieces of cheese-cloth, draping the excess over the sides (about 2 inches). Set aside.

Add 1 heaping cup of diced curd to the stainless steel bowl. With a pitcher or large ladle, cover the curd with hot salt water until it is completely submerged, then stir gently. When the curd has softened to a putty-like texture and begun to come together (1 to 2 minutes), drain in a colander and then return to the bowl and submerge the curd in a second bath until it is fully melted into a smooth mass (1 to 2 minutes). With gentle pressure, run a rubber spatula over the curd to smooth it out. Using your hands (it may be a bit warm), turn the ball of curd over on itself until it all has the same soft, smooth consistency.

Set the ball on a clean cutting board and push it out into a pancake shape approximately ¼ inch thick and 7 to 8 inches in diameter. Place it on the cheesecloth, allowing the excess to drape over the sides. Spoon in enough filling to fill ¾ of the form.

Close up the cheese by incrementally pulling up the sides into pleats and squeezing between the thumb and index finger so it adheres to itself. Pull up the cheesecloth over the burrata and hold firmly around the sealed top portion. Holding it with one hand, wrap the kitchen twine around the sealed top portion and tie tightly. Trim off excess cheese and cloth (the scraps are delicious), place the finished burrata in a plastic sandwich bag, and transfer to the baking dish of cool water. Let rest for 10 to 15 minutes. Repeat the process with the rest of the curd and filling.

Enjoy immediately, or refrigerate and use within 24 to 48 hours. For best texture, allow the cheese to warm slightly before serving.

Makes 6 burrata

To drink: Prosecco, Vermentino, Falaghina

ARTICHOKE SPREAD

Enjoying a good artichoke spread and appreciating the finer things are not mutually exclusive. In our deli, our artichoke spread resides and thrives amongst some of the finest cured meats, cheeses and olives in the world. True, it consists of simple ingredients that are easy to put together, but it has one thing going for it: it tastes really good.

Paired with Macrina's Apricot Nut Crostini or grilled bread, it will hold its own as an appetizer or a snack before the big game. Careful though—once you bring it to a friend's house for dinner, they will ask you to bring it again and again.

INGREDIENTS

3 14-ounce cans whole artichoke hearts

1 cup mayonnaise

5 ounces DeLaurenti Grated Blend or Parmigiano-Reggiano

1 to 2 garlic cloves, minced

5 to 10 dashes Tabasco sauce

1 teaspoon freshly ground black pepper

Squeeze excess water out of the individual artichoke hearts. In a food processor, pulse the artichoke hearts to a medium-fine texture.

Transfer the blended artichoke hearts to a large bowl and mix with the mayonnaise, cheese, garlic, Tabasco and black pepper.

CAPONATA

There are many variations to this classic Sicilian appetizer, but the one thing they all have in common is eggplant. If you think you don't like eggplant, this may change your mind. The sauce in this recipe makes it a customer favorite in our antipasto case. It has a touch of sweetness, in balance with the acidity of the vinegar and the spiciness of the cayenne. The recipe yields more sauce than you need, allowing you to freeze the rest. This will cut future prep time in half. Although we recommend that this dish be served alongside grilled bread as an antipasto, it also makes a fantastic topping for pizza and panini. It is best served at room temperature, loosened with a touch of olive oil.

INGREDIENTS

Parchment paper

2 medium eggplants, cleaned, ends trimmed, and cut into ½-inch dice

½ cup extra-virgin olive oil

2 tablespoons herbes de Provence

Salt and pepper

⅓ cup pine nuts, browned until fragrant (see page 48)

½ cup Sicilian pitted olives, quartered

½ cup roasted red peppers, diced

½ cup fresh Italian parsley, chopped

½ recipe Caponata Sauce (see below)

1 Macrina baguette, sliced, lightly oiled, and grilled or toasted

Caponata Sauce

3 garlic cloves, minced

3 tablespoons olive oil

¾ cup balsamic vinegar

6-ounce can tomato paste

¼ cup water, more as needed

¼ cup sugar

1½ teaspoons salt

½ teaspoon cayenne pepper, or to taste

First, prepare the Caponata Sauce: In a medium saucepan over medium-low heat, sauté the garlic in olive oil until fragrant, 1 to 2 minutes. Add the vinegar and reduce for 3 to 4 minutes. Add the tomato paste, water, sugar and salt, and simmer gently for 15 to 20 minutes, stirring frequently, until the ingredients come together as a glossy sauce. If the sauce is too thick, add a touch more water to loosen it up. Careful, the sauce may spit!

Remove from the heat, add the cayenne, and let cool. Use half the sauce for each batch of caponata, freezing the other half for future use.

Preheat the oven to 400°F. Line 2 sheet pans with parchment paper.

In a large bowl, toss the eggplant with olive oil and herbes de Provence. Season to taste with salt and pepper. Divide between the 2 sheet pans. Bake for 15 minutes, or until the eggplant is brown around the edges but not mushy. Remove from the oven and let cool completely.

When the eggplant has cooled, combine it with the browned pine nuts, olives, red peppers, parsley and half of the sauce. Gently toss (the amount of sauce may seem excessive, but the eggplant is very absorbent).

Place the caponata in a serving bowl and surround with grilled bread. If the caponata has been refrigerated, let it stand for a few minutes and add some olive oil to loosen it before serving.

To drink: Nero d'Avola, Northwest Sauvignon Blanc, Barbera

FETTUNTA *with* OLIO NOVELLO

Fettunta is a fall tradition in Italy, made to celebrate the new harvest of olive oil. Simple but delicious, it is essentially grilled bread with olive oil, garlic and sea salt. The bread, however, is only the vehicle. What makes this recipe and this tradition unique is the oil. Raw, green and pungent, the newly harvested oil is the truest expression of the tree's fruit. Not long ago, there was little local awareness of this great tradition. Fortunately, this is beginning to change. Every year at DeLaurenti, the quantity and variety of olio novello grow as people have the opportunity to appreciate the difference these oils can make. Whether you are making fettunta, finishing soups or enjoying a simple pasta, the addition of olio novello is often the difference between really good and great.

INGREDIENTS

1 baguette, or other good-quality rustic bread

2 garlic cloves, peeled and whole

½ cup olio novello, or other best-quality olive oil

Sea salt

Light a barbecue or turn on the broiler.

Slice the bread into rustic ½-inch pieces. Grill until golden. If you're using a broiler, place the bread in a single layer on a sheet pan and broil both sides until done to your liking.

Remove from the grill and lightly rub one side of each piece of bread with raw garlic. Lay the bread out on a serving platter and drizzle liberally with olio novello. Finish with sea salt.

Serves 4 to 6 as an appetizer

To drink: A young red—Lambrusco, Brachetto d'Acqui, Prosecco, Pinot Grigio

TUNA CARPACCIO *with* LEMON, CAPERS & PICKLED RED ONIONS

The obvious key to this dish is the quality of the fish. If you cannot get sushi-grade ahi tuna, do not attempt it. If you are lucky enough to work or live near the Pike Place Market, then you should make it often. When shopping for the fish, be sure to tell your fishmonger what you are doing with it—namely, that you have no intention of cooking it. This will ensure the best quality. The combination of ingredients in this recipe is a pure expression of the Pike Place Market. Tuna from Pike Place Fish, lemons and Italian parsley from Frank's or Sosio's, capers, olive oil and sea salt from DeLaurenti. Try this dish alongside a batch of Corona Beans (page 42) as a first course, or as a light dinner in the summertime.

INGREDIENTS

8 ounces best-quality ahi tuna

½ cup Pickled Red Onions (see below)

1 tablespoon plus 2 teaspoons capers

1 liberal tablespoon best-quality extra-virgin olive oil

Juice of ½ lemon

¼ teaspoon sea salt

1 healthy pinch of chopped fresh Italian parsley

Grilled bread, for serving

Pickled Red Onions

3 cups white wine vinegar

1 cup sugar

1 tablespoon kosher salt

3 bay leaves

5 allspice berries

2 dried arbol chiles

3 whole cloves

10 whole black peppercorns

2 medium red onions, thinly sliced

Thinly slice the tuna against the grain—it doesn't have to be perfect since you will be pounding it to the desired thickness. Place 3 or 4 pieces of tuna in between 2 pieces of plastic wrap, leaving plenty of space between.

With a meat mallet, gently pound the pieces until they are paper-thin. When they are held up to the light, you should be able to almost see through them. Repeat with the remaining tuna. If not using immediately, refrigerate the tuna, still in the plastic wrap, for up to 2 hours.

To serve, carefully peel the tuna away from the plastic and arrange in a single layer on a platter. Eight ounces of fish should almost cover a 12-by-12-inch platter.

Evenly distribute the red onions and capers over the tuna.

Drizzle with olive oil and lemon juice. Season with sea salt. Garnish with parsley. Serve with grilled bread.

Serves 4 to 6 as an appetizer

To drink: Chablis, Vermentino, Sauvignon Blanc

Pickled Red Onions

Combine all ingredients except the onions in a medium saucepan and bring to a boil. Add the onions and simmer for 1 minute.

Transfer the onions and pickling liquid to a separate container, cover, and refrigerate. Let sit overnight to let the flavors meld. These will keep in an airtight container in the fridge for weeks.

CORONA BEANS

These beautiful broad white beans are often misunderstood. Like most bean varieties, they take a little bit of planning and patience. Everyone who has ever picked up a container of dried beans asks themselves the same series of questions: Do I soak them? If so, for how long? When do I add the salt? Do I boil them? Simmer them? In what? And with what? Jeff Bergman, friend and local food col-league, helped us to unravel the mystery. A few years ago when we asked him to do a demo highlighting olio novello from Frescobaldi, he chose corona beans. They were unbelievable: tender, creamy and the perfect vehicle for the expression of the oil. We pestered him for his secret, and fortunately, he obliged. The process itself is very simple, but comes with one piece of advice: Pay attention.

INGREDIENTS

1 pound dried corona beans

4 good-quality bay leaves

8 garlic cloves, peeled

1 teaspoon whole black peppercorns

1 yellow onion, peeled and halved

3 tablespoons olive oil

1 tablespoon sea salt

Place the beans in a large pot with enough water to cover well. Discard any beans that float or ones that are damaged. Soak at room temperature for a minimum of 36 hours, and up to 48.

Drain and rinse the beans. Place in a large heavy-bottomed saucepan or Dutch oven. Cover with water.

Add the bay leaves, garlic, peppercorns, onions and olive oil.

Bring the beans to a boil slowly. Once the water has started to boil, reduce the heat until it just barely simmers. You should see only a ripple.

Cook uncovered for 2 to 4 hours, depending on the age of the beans. After 2 hours, start testing the beans every 15 minutes. They are done when they are very tender throughout.

Remove from the heat. Add the sea salt to the water and let the beans cool in the cooking liquid until tepid.

Store the beans in the refrigerator for up to a week in the cooking liquid.

When you're ready to use the beans, rinse and combine them with your favorite ingredients.

Serves 8 to 12

Note: It's a great idea to double this recipe. These beans keep well and are excellent to have at your disposal.

With Olio Novello, Lemon and Italian Parsley

4 cups cooked corona beans

1 cup olio novello, or other best-quality extra-virgin olive oil

Grated zest and juice of ½ lemon

¼ cup chopped fresh Italian parsley

Salt and pepper to taste

Combine all the ingredients and mix. The bottom layer
of beans should be almost fully submerged in oil.

Other additions:

Shaved red onion

Best-quality canned tuna

Baby arugula

Halved sweet cherry tomatoes

Capers

Fresh herbs of your choice

To drink: Gavi, Bourgogne Blanc

TROFIE *with* PESTO, POTATOES
& HARICOTS VERTS

Trofie is a traditional Ligurian cut of pasta that resembles a twisted matchstick. Pat had his initial encounter with this dish while in Italy for the first time. He was roaming Portofino with his friend Mario Gelmini in search of a late lunch. The restaurant Mario poked his head into said they were closed, but they agreed to seat them. They received no menu, just the chef's idea of a latecomers' lunch. They had grilled scampi and this pasta. The pesto was unforgettable, as was the entire experience. You might note that there are two starches in this recipe: pasta and potatoes. The strict traditionalist may say this is unacceptable, but if the Ligurians serve their trofie al pesto with potatoes, we can too. It is great warm, even on a hot day, or served cold as a salad.

INGREDIENTS

1 cup haricots verts or other thin green beans

8 ounces small red potatoes

1 package trofie pasta (8.8 ounces)

5 to 6 tablespoons Basil Pesto (see below)

Salt

Parmigiano-Reggiano, for serving

Basil Pesto

2 bunches fresh basil leaves – about 4 cups
    loosely packed - blanched

½ cup extra-virgin olive oil

⅓ cup pine nuts, lightly browned (see page 48)

2 tablespoons grated Parmigiano-Reggiano

1 tablespoon grated Pecorino Romano

1 garlic clove

½ teaspoon kosher salt, or to taste

Bring 6 quarts of water to a boil with 2 tablespoons kosher salt.

Prepare an ice bath by filling a large mixing bowl halfway with equal parts water and ice.

Blanch the beans in the pasta water until tender but still crisp, about 1 to 2 minutes, depending on the size of the beans. Remove with a strainer and transfer to the ice bath, dry, and set aside.

Cook the whole potatoes in the pasta water for 5 to 6 minutes, or until fork-tender. Remove, let cool, and halve.

Cook the pasta until al dente according to the package instructions, reserving ½ cup of the pasta water.

Warm a large mixing bowl. In the bowl, combine the hot pasta with the beans, potatoes, pesto and reserved pasta water. Add salt to taste.

Divide among 4 warmed pasta bowls. Serve immediately with grated Parmigiano-Reggiano.

Serves 4

To drink: Vermentino, Verdicchio di Jesi, Pigato

Basil Pesto

If you want your pesto to taste good and look good, do not skip the blanching step. It will ensure that your sauce stays a vibrant green in your pasta this evening or in your freezer all winter. Bring 1 quart of water to a boil in a pasta pot and prepare an ice bath. Place the basil leaves in a colander. Blanch for 10 seconds and then submerge in the ice bath. Lay out the leaves on a towel and blot dry. In a food processor, blend all the ingredients until the sauce is smooth but still has a little bit of texture. Use more or less olive oil to control the consistency.

PAPPARDELLE *with* CHANTERELLES & GUANCIALE

This is a great pasta for the fall, when you start thinking about drinking red wine again. Justin Lyon, our former café manager, made this dish at our first family dinner. The only ingredient he stepped out of the store to get was the mushrooms. At the time, we were in the chanterelle window: that period between the end of *September and the first frost when the mushrooms pop out of the ground and into the market stalls. There aren't many ways to improve on their flavor, but Justin found one by adding guanciale (cured pork jowl). Be sure to use the pasta water at the end and don't skip the drizzle of oil—these steps ensure a silky sauce.*

INGREDIENTS

4 ounces guanciale, thinly sliced into matchsticks

1 tablespoon good-quality extra-virgin olive oil, plus more for drizzling

1 small shallot, minced

¾ pound chanterelles, cleaned and coarsely chopped

1 cup chicken stock

1 tablespoon chopped fresh chives

1 cup heavy cream

Salt and pepper

1 pound fresh egg pappardelle

¾ cup grated Parmigiano-Reggiano, plus more for garnish

2 tablespoons chopped fresh Italian parsley, plus a pinch for garnish

Bring 6 quarts of water to a boil with 2 tablespoons salt.

In a large skillet, sauté the guanciale in olive oil over medium heat until lightly crisp, about 2 minutes. Remove with a slotted spoon and drain on paper towels.

Add the shallots to the pan with the reserved guanciale fat and cook until soft, about 1 minute. Add the chanterelles and cook until the moisture has been released and the edges begin to brown, 2 to 3 minutes. Add the chicken stock and chives, and cook until the liquid is reduced by half. Add the cream and simmer until the sauce coats the back of a wooden spoon. Add the reserved guanciale and season the sauce with salt and pepper to taste. Turn the heat to low.

Cook the pasta for 2 minutes, or until al dente, then reserve 1 cup of pasta water and drain.

Add the hot pasta to the sauce, as well as ¾ cup cheese, ½ cup pasta water and 2 tablespoons parsley. If the sauce is too thick, add pasta water to reach the desired consistency. Cook over medium-low heat to reduce for 1 minute.

Remove from the heat, divide the pasta among 4 bowls, and drizzle with olive oil. Garnish with cheese and parsley. Serve immediately.

Serves 4

To drink: Barbera d'Alba

TRENNE SICILIANA

This pasta is a good reason to keep a well-stocked pantry. Things you should have: quality pasta, tomatoes, red pepper flakes, tomato paste, tuna, olives, capers and olive oil. The quality of ingredients is very important in this recipe. We prefer Rustichella d'Abruzzo trenne. This shape resembles a triangular penne that is a touch more delicate. Its size and texture work perfectly with the sauce. DOP San Marzano tomatoes and either Spanish, Portuguese or good-quality domestic troll-caught tuna are not optional. Lesser-known Saracena olives are to southern Italy what Kalamatas are to southern Greece. Their full flavor and buttery texture is superior. Finally, be sure to use good-quality capers, in brine or salt, and your best extra-virgin olive oil for drizzling.

INGREDIENTS

3 garlic cloves, sliced thin

1 teaspoon red pepper flakes, more if you prefer it spicier

3 tablespoons extra-virgin olive oil, plus more for drizzling

28-ounce can DOP San Marzano tomatoes, with juice

½ cup pitted Saracena olives

2 tablespoons capers

2 teaspoons tomato paste

Salt and pepper

1 pound dried trenne or other short cut of pasta

2 6-ounce cans best-quality tuna packed in oil, flaked

½ cup chopped fresh Italian parsley, plus more for garnish

Bring 6 quarts of water to a boil with 2 tablespoons salt.

In a large skillet over medium-low heat, sauté the garlic and red pepper flakes in olive oil until softened and fragrant, 1 to 2 minutes, being careful to not let the garlic burn.

Crush the tomatoes by hand and add to the pan. Bring to a simmer and cook for 10 minutes, until slightly reduced. Add the olives, capers and tomato paste. Simmer for 2 minutes. Season to taste with salt and pepper.

Cook the pasta according to the package instructions. Just before the pasta is al dente, add the tuna and parsley to the sauce and heat through. Combine the hot pasta with the sauce.

Finish with a drizzle of olive oil, garnish with the remaining parsley, and serve immediately.

Serves 4

To drink: Nero d'Avola, Primitivo, Italian Rosé

LINGUINE GAMBERI *in* SALSA ROSSA

A winter's dilemma: You want the comfort of a hearty red sauce, but something from the sea is calling you. Problem solved. In a perfect world, this recipe should be made with reserved acqua pazza (page 82) as your stock. That said, good-quality seafood stock works great. A few tips: When making the red sauce, double or triple the recipe to have extra in the freezer. Keep some of the sauce in its rustic form for other uses, but don't skip the puree step for this particular pasta. The smooth texture works well. Last, if you have the luxury of living or working near the Pike Place Market, finding good shellfish is not a problem. If you don't and can't find them, wait until you have the time to come to the Market before making this pasta.

INGREDIENTS

1 cup chopped sweet onion

3 tablespoons olive oil

3 garlic cloves, thinly sliced

½ cup chopped carrot

½ cup chopped celery

1 tablespoon minced fresh thyme

28-ounce can DOP San Marzano tomatoes, with juice

Salt and pepper

1 pound linguine

1 pound shrimp, peeled, deveined and rinsed

1 teaspoon red pepper flakes, more if you prefer it spicier

1½ cups fish stock

½ cup dry white wine

Extra-virgin olive oil, for garnish

Fresh Italian parsley, chopped, for garnish

In a large skillet, cook the onions in 2 tablespoons olive oil over medium-low heat, covered, for 10 minutes. Stir occasionally, being careful to not let the onions burn. Add the garlic, carrots, celery and thyme, and cook until softened, about 5 minutes. Crush the tomatoes by hand, add to the pan, and simmer for 30 minutes. Add salt and pepper to taste. Transfer the sauce to a blender or food processor and puree. Return the sauce to the pan and set aside.

Bring 6 quarts of water to a boil with 2 tablespoons salt. Add the linguine and cook according to the package instructions. Save 1 cup of pasta water, then drain the pasta.

While the pasta cooks, season the shrimp with salt and pepper. In a separate skillet over medium heat, sauté the shrimp in the remaining olive oil and red pepper flakes until almost done, about 3 minutes. They should still be a bit opaque in the center. Transfer the shrimp to a plate and set aside.

Add the stock and wine to the shrimp skillet and cook to reduce over medium-high heat for 3 minutes. Ladle the red sauce into the stock/wine mixture until it has the consistency of a thin soup—you may have a little red sauce left over. Add the shrimp and warm gently.

Add the hot pasta to the sauce and mix. Add pasta water for the desired consistency—it should be loose and saucy. Divide the pasta among 4 plates and garnish with olive oil and parsley. Serve immediately.

Serves 4

To drink: Rosé

FUSILLI *with* CHANTERELLES & SAGE
in SUGO ROSA

If you lament the passing of summer, the smell of chanterelles being sautéed in olive oil and butter can help. This recipe comes from Mario Gelmini, friend and owner of Caffè Senso Unico in Seattle. He simply calls it "the chanterelles in the pink sauce." This pasta is a great expression of fall in the Northwest, although he would never call it that. It is simply what you do when the mushrooms and sage are perfect, it's too cold to eat outside, and you feel like a glass of red wine. However you say it, the best Italian food in Seattle is at Mario's house.

INGREDIENTS

1 pound dried fusilli

1 shallot, minced

1 tablespoon butter

2 tablespoons olive oil

¾ pound chanterelle mushrooms, cleaned
  and coarsely chopped

3 tablespoons coarsely chopped fresh sage

1 cup chicken stock

4 tablespoons tomato paste

1 cup heavy cream

Salt and pepper

Parmigiano-Reggiano, for serving

Bring 6 quarts of water to a boil with 2 tablespoons salt. Add the pasta.

While the pasta is cooking, sauté the shallots in a large skillet over medium heat in butter and olive oil until translucent, about 2 minutes.

Add the mushrooms and sage, and continue to cook for 2 to 3 minutes. The mushrooms should give off some moisture and begin to brown. Add the chicken stock and tomato paste, and cook to reduce the liquid by a quarter. Turn the heat to medium-low, add the cream, and simmer, stirring, for 2 to 3 minutes. The sauce should be a rosy pink. Season to taste with salt and pepper.

When the pasta is al dente, reserve 1 cup of pasta water, then drain the pasta. Transfer the hot pasta to the skillet and toss. If the sauce is too thick, add pasta water to achieve the desired consistency. Divide among 4 warmed pasta bowls and top with grated Parmigiano-Reggiano.

Serves 4

To drink: Nebbiolo, Barbaresco, Schiava

BOLOGNESE

Although there are as many Bolognese recipes as there are Italian restaurants, we wanted to include one of our own. This one comes from our chef, Garrett Abel. There are a few keys to this dish: First, using a variety of pancetta and prosciutto ends that have been pulsed in a food processor really adds depth to the sauce. Second, browning the meats is important. To do this, you need space in your pan—if it's too crowded, the meat will steam. Work in batches if your pan is not big enough. Last, finishing with an immersion blender will help to achieve a textured sauce that still clings well to pasta. Needless to say, if you are going to the trouble of making a sauce that takes more than three hours, doubling the recipe is a good idea. This will give you plenty of sauce to freeze and use with a variety of pasta shapes.

INGREDIENTS

3 medium onions, finely diced

4 tablespoons olive oil

2 tablespoons unsalted butter

4 medium carrots, finely diced

5 celery stalks, finely diced

¾ pound pancetta and/or prosciutto ends, finely diced
    and pulsed in a food processor

1 pound ground pork

1 pound ground beef

8 ounces chicken livers, finely minced (optional,
    but better when included)

1 cup dry white wine

2 cups chicken stock

2 cups whole milk or cream

2 24-ounce jars passata (uncooked tomato puree
    strained of seeds and skin)

Salt and freshly ground pepper

Freshly grated nutmeg

In a large sauté pan over medium-high heat, sauté the onions in olive oil and butter until translucent, about 5 minutes. Add the carrots and celery, and cook until softened, about 6 minutes. Transfer the vegetables from the sauté pan to a large Dutch oven or heavy-bottomed pot.

In the same sauté pan, cook the pancetta/prosciutto until it is starting to crisp, but not burn. Push to the back of the pan, exposing a hot surface. Add the pork and beef to the hot spot and brown, crumbling with the back of a wooden spoon. Push back and repeat the browning process with the chicken livers. When done, add all the meat to the Dutch oven.

Deglaze the sauté pan with the wine, scraping up any browned bits. Let it cook for 1 minute and then transfer to the pot of meat and vegetables.

Add the chicken stock, milk/cream and passata to the pot. Stir and bring to a simmer over low heat. Cook, uncovered, for 3 hours, stirring occasionally and adding a touch of stock if the mixture is too thick.

When the sauce is done, insert an immersion blender (you can also use a food processor) and pulse to break up any pieces of ground beef/pork that have stuck together. Add salt, pepper and nutmeg to taste.

Toss with your pasta of choice, using approximately 2 cups of sauce per pound of pasta.

Makes 6 cups

To drink: Sangiovese di Romagna, Nebbiolo, Barbera

POTATO GNOCCHI

There are few things more satisfying than perfect, delicate pillows of homemade gnocchi. Unfortunately, there are also few things worse than the dense and gummy replicas that some people are accustomed to having. Because the experience of eating the real thing is so much better, many people are inclined to think that it must take years of training, hard-to-find ingredients, or hours and hours of prep. Nothing could be further from the truth. There is only one rule: Gnocchi are to be made at home, not purchased. Once you commit to this, you are a russet potato, some flour, a few eggs and a pinch of salt away from glory. A few things to note before you get started: We found that baking the potatoes produced a lighter, fluffier result. Smooth and simple sauces work best with the delicate texture of the gnocchi. And last, preparing homemade gnocchi is an interactive affair. Be sure you have friends or family around to share in the effort.

INGREDIENTS

2 pounds (about 3 medium) russet potatoes

3 large egg yolks

2 tablespoons salt

2 cups all-purpose flour, plus more for dusting

Preheat the oven to 400°F. Pierce the potatoes and bake for about 1 hour, or until tender throughout.

Bring 6 quarts of water to a boil with 2 tablespoons kosher salt.

When the potatoes are cool enough to handle, peel and pass them through a potato ricer or food mill into a large bowl. Add the egg yolks and salt, and stir until the dough has a smooth consistency.

Add the flour slowly in ½-cup increments. When the dough begins to come together, transfer it to a floured work surface. Knead it gently, dusting with more flour, until the dough doesn't stick to your hands.

Cut off a baseball-size piece and gently roll it out into a ½-inch-thick rope. Cut into ½-inch pieces and carefully transfer to a floured cookie sheet in a single layer. For ridged gnocchi: Using your thumb, press lightly and roll the pieces against a gnocchi board or the tines of a fork to create a depression on one side and a ridge on the other. Repeat until finished.

At this point, the dough should be cooked immediately or frozen. If freezing, lay out gnocchi in a single layer on a sheet pan, loosely cover with plastic wrap, and place in the freezer for about 3 hours, then transfer to a ziplock bag. Gnocchi can be stored in the freezer for up to a month.

Working in batches, cook the gnocchi in the boiling water until they float, about 1 minute. Remove with a slotted spoon and serve with the desired sauce.

Serves 4

Here are three simple sauce options to try with these gnocchi, or any other pasta of your choice. Each recipe will dress approximately 1 pound of pasta.

Gorgonzola Sauce

2 cups heavy cream
4 ounces Mountain Gorgonzola, crumbled
3 tablespoons freshly grated Parmigiano-Reggiano
Salt and pepper

In a medium saucepan over medium heat, bring the cream to a simmer. Stirring occasionally, reduce the cream until it coats the back of a wooden spoon, about 10 minutes. Turn the heat to low and whisk in the Gorgonzola, Parmigiano-Reggiano, and salt and pepper to taste.

When the gnocchi are ready, toss with the sauce, add salt and pepper to taste, and serve immediately.

To drink: White Vin de Savoie, Dry Riesling, Valpolicella

Butter and Sage Sauce

½ cup (1 stick) unsalted butter
12 sage leaves
½ cup grated Parmigiano-Reggiano, plus more for serving
Salt and pepper

In a medium saucepan over medium heat, melt the butter until it begins to brown, but not burn, about 1 to 2 minutes. Remove from the heat and add the sage.

When the gnocchi are floating, return the sauce to the heat. Toss the finished gnocchi with the sauce and a touch of reserved pasta water and simmer for 1 minute. Remove from the heat, add the cheese and salt and pepper to taste, and serve immediately with more Parmigiano-Reggiano.

To drink: Soave, Vermentino from the Piedmont

Tomato Cream Sauce

2 cups heavy cream
3 tablespoons tomato paste
Salt and pepper
Parmigiano-Reggiano, for serving

In a medium saucepan over medium heat, bring the cream to a simmer. Stirring occasionally, reduce the cream until it coats the back of a wooden spoon, about 10 minutes. Turn the heat to low and add the tomato paste, stirring until it is fully incorporated. Add salt and pepper to taste.

When the gnocchi are ready, toss with the sauce and a touch of reserved pasta water and simmer for 1 minute. Add more salt to taste and serve immediately with grated Parmigiano-Reggiano.

To drink: Pinot Bianco, Dolcetto

RICOTTA GNOCCHI

Everything you love about potato gnocchi without the potato. A touch lighter and more tender than traditional gnocchi, these dumplings are a delicate balance of fresh whole-milk ricotta and eggs, with just enough flour to hold them together. As you may suspect, the centerpiece of this recipe is the ricotta, and not all ricotta is created equal. As with many ingredients that you can find everywhere, most of what you find is not the best quality. At DeLaurenti, we sell an award-winning ricotta from the Calabro Cheese Corp. It has a light and soft texture, and a wonderful milky sweetness that is perfect for *both sweet and savory applications. Without it, this dish is not worth making. A few pointers: First, even if the cheese does not feel exceptionally wet, do not skip the draining step. Too much moisture in the cheese will make your gnocchi fall apart, or force you to use too much flour, which ruins the light texture. Second, it's okay if your gnocchi are not uniform. Rustic is good. Last, as with potato gnocchi, simple and smooth sauces are best. Good olive oil, butter or tomato cream sauces highlight the soft texture of the pasta.*

INGREDIENTS

12 ounces fresh ricotta, well drained

2 large eggs

2 large egg yolks

4 ounces grated Parmigiano-Reggiano, plus more for garnish

Salt

About 1 cup all-purpose flour

2 tablespoons salted butter or good-quality olive oil

In a medium-sized bowl, combine the ricotta, eggs, egg yolks, half of the Parmigiano-Reggiano and a pinch of salt. Mix well with a wooden spoon.

Gradually add flour until the mixture comes together as a dough that does not stick to your hands—about ¾ cup (you may need more or less flour, depending on the amount of moisture in the ricotta).

Flour your hands well and portion the dough into hazelnut-sized dumplings. Gently roll the dumplings between your palms to shape. Place the gnocchi on a floured cookie sheet. If freezing, loosely cover them with plastic wrap and place in the freezer. Once the gnocchi are firm enough to handle, transfer to ziplock bags and store for up to a month.

Bring 4 quarts of water to a boil with 2 tablespoons kosher salt.

Over medium-low heat in a medium skillet, melt the butter or heat olive oil, being careful to not let it burn.

Add the gnocchi to the boiling water and stir gently. When they float to the top, in about 1 minute, remove with a slotted spoon and transfer to the skillet. Add ½ cup pasta water and the remaining Parmigiano-Reggiano and simmer until the sauce thickens.

Divide the gnocchi among 4 to 6 warmed pasta bowls, garnish with additional Parmigiano-Reggiano, and serve immediately.

Serves 4 to 6 (makes about 50 gnocchi)

Spinach and Ricotta Gnocchi

Add a 10-ounce package of frozen spinach (thawed and squeezed of all liquid) when you combine the ricotta, eggs, Parmigiano-Reggiano and salt. Use only as much flour as needed to achieve a soft dough.

To drink: Unoaked Chardonnay, Nebbiolo

ENTRÉES

The Seasons – Let them do the work for you. Eat and prepare according to what they provide you. Do less, pay less, and get better results.

The Great Contradiction – Take the food you eat seriously, go to great lengths to make it good, care about it, think it's really important, but please, don't take yourself too seriously. It's just food.

Aristotle's Rule – A friend to all is a friend to none. This applies to food as well. Just because you have a lot of ingredients, that does not mean you have to use them all. At least not all at once. If you have to think too hard about whether something belongs, it probably doesn't.

Hurt the Ones You Love – Experimenting with new recipes is great, but do it on the people closest to you. They are more forgiving and more honest, and will still love you afterward.

Simple Food Is Complex – We are the fortunate beneficiaries of hundreds of years of culinary skill, hard work, tradition and human ingenuity. Take a moment to appreciate the long list of wonderful things that grace our tables. The onion, the carrot, the lamb, the wine, the cheese, the bread: these things did not happen by accident. Each has its own specific history. Enjoy them without reservation, but also with great gratitude.

Go with What You Know – The more people you invite to dinner, the fewer things you should attempt for the first time.

Ask – Trust your cheesemonger, your produce guy and your butcher.

Starch – Civilizations are supported by it. Your body needs it. No more than two on a plate. Good bread, pasta and grains bring too much joy and too much health to be left off the plate.

Bread – Bread is an art *and* a science. Buy it from an artisan bakery; their care and knowledge will prove every time that there is bread, and then there is BREAD!

Salad Before vs. Salad After – In Italy, you may not have a choice, but here you do. Thankfully, there is no right answer here, and you are no less refined for choosing before.

It's Not Just How You Start, It's Also How You Finish – Don't skip the final touches. Fresh herbs, lemon, olive oil, sea salt, pepper, bacon—something silky, crunchy, smoky, spicy or bright—these are the things that often separate the forgettable from the remarkable.

An Oil for All Occasions – There are the oils you use when it doesn't matter, and the oils you use when it really does. Both matter. You should have a minimum of two: one for cooking and one for finishing. The maximum number of oils you should have is a question of economics, usage and storage. Strive to cover the flavor continuum from buttery, smooth and fruity to raw and peppery.

Good Canned Tomatoes – One of the greatest culinary and technological advancements of all time. It took a special person, with a passion for tomatoes, to come up with this. Whoever it was, we all owe this person great appreciation every time we make a red sauce in the month of January.

The Inside of a Lemon and the Outside of a Lemon – Most people know what the inside of a lemon can do, but fewer people harness the power of its underutilized exterior. Zest can provide punch that juice cannot. Fortunately, this is not an either/or proposition; utilize both.

All Butter Is Not Created Equal – In a recipe or on a baguette, the better the butter, the better the results. And always keep some out on the counter.

BRAISED SHORT RIBS *with* POLENTA

Braising is a magical thing. It turns otherwise tough and less palatable cuts of meat into things of beauty. The process is surprisingly simple: Brown the ribs and add your aromatics. Unlock the flavor with wine, stock and herbs, and put the whole thing in the oven for a few hours. It couldn't be easier, and the payoff is immense. An added benefit of this dish is that it can all be done in advance. This makes it *the perfect option for cool-weather gatherings when you would rather be spending time with friends or family than cooking. We suggest serving these ribs on a bed of creamy polenta; however, this recipe also doubles as braised short rib ragu. When the ribs are done, pick off the meat, combine with the sauce, toss with fresh buttered pappardelle, and finish with Parmigiano-Reggiano.*

INGREDIENTS

3½ pounds short ribs, cut in 4- to 5-inch sections

Salt and freshly ground pepper

3 tablespoons olive oil

1 cup diced onion

1 cup diced celery

1 cup diced carrot

2 garlic cloves, chopped

2 tablespoons tomato paste

5 cups beef stock

2 tablespoons fresh rosemary, chopped

1½ cups dry red wine

1 batch of polenta (page 72)

Fresh Italian parsley, for garnish

Preheat the oven to 300°F.

Season the ribs liberally with salt and pepper.

In a large, heavy-bottomed sauté pan or Dutch oven, heat the olive oil over high heat until smoking. Working in batches, cook the ribs until deep brown on all sides, including the ends, about 15 minutes total. Set the ribs aside on a separate plate.

Reduce the heat to medium and add the onions, celery, carrots and garlic. Cook until softened, about 3 to 4 minutes. Season to taste with salt and pepper. Add the tomato paste and brown for 1 minute.

Add the beef stock, rosemary and wine, and bring to a boil, using a wooden spoon to scrape up any browned bits stuck to the bottom of the pan. Return the ribs and excess juices to the Dutch oven, cover with a lid or foil, and place in the oven for 1½ to 2 hours, or until the meat is tender and falling off the bone.

Transfer the ribs to a separate platter and tent with foil. Let the sauce cool slightly and then skim off the fat (allowing 30 to 45 minutes makes this step easier). Place the sauce on high heat and reduce, skimming the froth occasionally, until the sauce coats the back of a wooden spoon. If the sauce is too thick, add a touch more stock to reach the desired consistency. Reduce the heat to low, adjust the seasoning, and return the ribs to the pot to warm through.

Place a scoop of polenta in each of 4 warmed pasta bowls. Rest a rib or two on top of the polenta, add some sauce, garnish with parsley, and serve immediately.

Serves 4

Note: This can be made a day or two ahead. Separate the ribs from the sauce before refrigerating them both. Skim the fat from the sauce before returning the ribs to the pot. Combine, cover, and reheat in a 300°F oven until warmed through. You can make the polenta while heating the ribs.

To drink: Châteauneuf-du-Pape, Barbaresco, Morgon, Nebbiolo

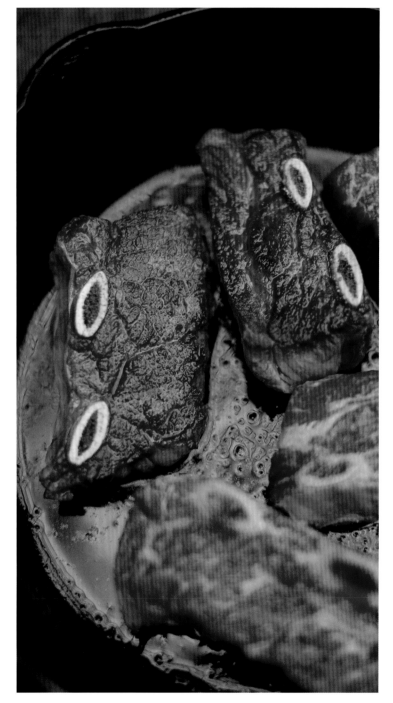

POLENTA

Polenta is as basic a recipe as there is in Italian cooking. That noted, it's very difficult to get two people to agree on the best recipe. It seems that everyone who has a polenta recipe operates with their own set of absolutes. There are a number of variables: water, broth, butter, cheese, fine, medium, coarse. When we asked the staff for their opinions on polenta, we got as many answers as employees. In the end, we simply couldn't agree on one polenta recipe. Thus, we have included two. One thing we all could agree on, however, is that polenta plays an indispensable role in the kitchen. There is perhaps no better backdrop for braised and grilled meats, sausages or vegetables. The key here is the basic ratio of 4 cups of liquid to 1 cup of polenta. You have likely heard stories about having to stir polenta for 45 minutes to get it right. There is no need to do that. Follow these recipes and you'll make polenta far more often.

INGREDIENTS

3 cups water

1 cup whole milk

1 cup coarse polenta

1 tablespoon unsalted butter

2 teaspoons salt

⅓ cup grated Parmigiano-Reggiano

Or

3 cups water

1 cup chicken broth

1 cup coarse polenta

1 tablespoon unsalted butter

2 teaspoons salt

⅓ cup grated Parmigiano-Reggiano

¼ cup heavy whipping cream

In a high-sided saucepan or Dutch oven, heat the water and milk (or broth) to a simmer and whisk in the polenta. Cook over medium heat, stirring continuously with a wooden spoon, for 10 to 12 minutes, or until the polenta begins to pull away from the sides of the pan. Stir in the butter, salt and Parmigiano-Reggiano. If you are using the broth recipe, stir in the cream until incorporated.

Note: If you are using medium polenta, cook for 8 to 9 minutes; for fine, 7 to 8 minutes. For firmer polenta, use a 3-to-1 ratio of liquid to polenta.

Serves 4

To drink: Chianti Classico, Rosso di Montepulciano

CHICKEN & SAUCE

There are a few dishes we all make that always hit the spot. We don't have to think about the recipe—we know it by heart. Everyone likes it and there are never leftovers. This is such a dish. It is a great recipe for a dinner party or a Monday night. The heart of this recipe is the caper/lemon/butter combo. This trio is also fantastic with pork, veal or fish. The best part is the remaining sauce that requires mopping up with your favorite Macrina loaf. The dish is not exotic and doesn't have an Italian name—it's simply chicken and sauce.

INGREDIENTS

2 whole boneless, skinless chicken breasts,
    cut in half horizontally

3 tablespoons butter

1 tablespoon olive oil

3 garlic cloves, sliced thin

1 medium shallot, diced

1 cup dry white wine

Juice of 1 large lemon (or 2 small)

½ cup capers

1 tablespoon fresh rosemary leaves, chopped

¼ cup heavy cream

Salt and pepper

Trim the chicken of extra fat and pound to an even thickness, about ¾ inch.

Melt the butter and olive oil in a large sauté pan over medium-high heat. Add the chicken and sauté for 4 to 5 minutes on each side. Remove the chicken to a dish and tent with foil.

Add the garlic and shallots to the pan and sauté for 1 to 2 minutes. Add the wine and continue to cook until reduced by a third.

Add the lemon juice, capers, rosemary and cream. Cook for several minutes, stirring, then add salt and pepper to taste. Return the chicken and any drippings to the pan, and stir to coat over low heat for 4 minutes.

Serve alongside roasted potatoes and your favorite grilled vegetable.

Serves 4

To drink: White Burgundy, Soave

PROSCIUTTO-WRAPPED
PORK TENDERLOIN *with* ROSEMARY

This is a simple and delicious recipe for summer barbecue nights. It can be prepped ahead of time, cooks quickly, and is beautiful when presented. We are often asked which prosciutto we recommend for cooking. It might be more economical to use a less expensive variety, but in this recipe, as with most, there is no substitute for Parma *or San Daniele. You can control the salt more easily, and it simply tastes better. Be sure to have the prosciutto cut just thicker than paper-thin—you want it to achieve a nice crackly texture on the grill without falling apart.*

INGREDIENTS

1½-pound pork tenderloin

Salt and freshly ground pepper

4 ounces prosciutto di Parma, sliced

3 to 4 sprigs fresh rosemary

Kitchen twine

Light a gas grill or charcoal fire.

Remove the silver skin from the tenderloin. Season liberally with salt and pepper.

On a clean work surface, lay out 4 to 5 slices of prosciutto, slightly overlapping lengthwise. The amount of prosciutto you use will depend on the size of the tenderloin.

Tuck the tail end of the tenderloin over about 2 inches to ensure even cooking. Lay the meat down on one edge of the prosciutto, 1 inch from the end. Place the rosemary sprigs lengthwise alongside the loin like a splint, leaving the stalk ends slightly exposed. Wrap the loin and rosemary with the prosciutto and tie snugly with twine.

Place on the barbecue on medium-high heat and grill, turning occasionally, until the internal temperature is 145°F. Let rest for 5 minutes.

Pull the rosemary stalks out and remove the twine. Carve the pork and serve with polenta and grilled vegetables, or over a cold arugula salad.

Serves 3 to 4, depending on the size of the tenderloin

To drink: Pinot Noir, Rosé, Dry Riesling

SEARED SALMON *with* MORELS
& GRILLED ASPARAGUS

This dish can be enjoyed anytime, but it's best in June, when morels first make an appearance, Washington asparagus is in full swing, and Copper River salmon season has arrived. The fact that these three things all reach their peak at the same time, in the same place, is nothing short of perfect. But wait, it gets better. Did we mention that it doesn't get dark until 9 p.m. and the new summer releases of rosé have hit the shelves at DeLaurenti? This recipe involves a very *simple and essential technique for cooking fish: pan searing and then finishing in the oven. There are conflicting philosophies on how to get a good crust on your fish and still cook it perfectly. The secret? Don't flip it, don't touch it, and pull it out just before you think it's done. If there isn't a small part of you that is still wondering whether your fish is done, it's too well done.*

INGREDIENTS

1½ to 2 pounds salmon fillet

1 bunch of asparagus

2 tablespoons olive oil, plus more for coating the asparagus

Salt and freshly ground pepper

8 ounces fresh morel mushrooms

⅓ cup chicken stock

1 tablespoon unsalted butter

4 tablespoons canola oil

Preheat the oven to 400°F.

Remove the skin and pin bones from the salmon and divide into 4 equal pieces. Rinse and pat dry. Transfer the fillets to a plate and put them in the fridge for a few minutes, uncovered. This will help in getting a good crust on the fish.

Snap the bottom off one piece of asparagus, noting where it breaks. Cut the rest of the bunch to the same length. Transfer to a roasting pan, lightly coat with olive oil, and season liberally with salt and pepper. Set aside.

Trim the stalks and any soft areas from the morels. Rinse and pat dry. In a medium skillet over medium-high heat, sauté the mushrooms in 2 tablespoons olive oil until softened but still al dente, approximately 5 minutes. Season to taste with salt and pepper.

Add the chicken stock to the pan and cook to reduce for 1 to 2 minutes. Remove from the heat and stir in the butter. Set the sauce aside, off the heat, while you cook the fish and asparagus.

If you're using a barbecue, cook the asparagus on high heat until the spears develop a nice char, but are still firm. If using the oven, roast at 450°F, occasionally shaking the pan to give all the spears the same nice char.

In an ovenproof skillet over high heat, warm the canola oil until just smoking. Season the salmon fillets with salt and place in the pan, at least 3 to 4 inches apart, skinned side up. Do not overcrowd the pan. Divide the fish between 2 skillets if the pan is not big enough. Sear for 1 to 2 minutes, until a crust forms.

Without flipping the fish, transfer the pan to the 400°F oven and bake until the fish is cooked to taste, about 3 to 5 minutes, depending on the thickness.

Place the morels and sauce back on the heat to warm through.

Transfer the grilled asparagus to serving plates or a large platter. When the fish is done, flip the fillets and place crust-side up on top of the asparagus. Spoon the morel and butter sauce over the fish and serve immediately.

Serves 4

To drink: Pinot Noir, Lagrein, Refosco, Rosé from Provence

STABBED CHICKEN *with* GREEK OREGANO

Greek culture has given us many important things: democracy, philosophy, the Olympic Games and great theater. One essential contribution that is often left off this list is the chicken. This recipe, more of a technique, comes to us from Matt's good friend Peter Lambros of Missoula, Montana. He got it from a small but famous chicken place in southern Athens. No basting, no bricks, no butter and no injections. All you need is a good-quality chicken, salt, Greek oregano, a lemon and a hot grill.

INGREDIENTS

8 whole best-quality chicken legs, trimmed of extra fat

Sea salt

Freshly ground black pepper

¼ cup good-quality dried Greek oregano leaves

3 lemons, 2 cut into wedges and 1 juiced

Extra-virgin olive oil, for drizzling

Place the chicken legs on a sheet pan. With a knife or sharp fork, stab each leg repeatedly on both sides. Season liberally with sea salt, cover with plastic wrap, and refrigerate for 4 hours, or up to 24.

Light a charcoal fire or turn a gas grill to medium-high.

Place the chicken on the grill, flesh side down. Cover and grill, turning occasionally, until the pieces are golden brown on all sides (20 to 25 minutes) and cooked through.

Before removing it from the grill, season the chicken liberally on all sides with sea salt, pepper and oregano. Turn the heat to low or move the chicken to a cooler part of the grill and let it rest for 5 minutes. The chicken should be well browned and tender, and the skin should be shrinking from the bone.

Transfer the chicken to a platter and garnish with lemon wedges. Finish with the juice of 1 lemon and a drizzle of olive oil just before serving.

Serves 6

To drink: Vernaccia di San Gimignano, Piedmont Chardonnay, Jurançon Sec

SPOT PRAWNS *in* CRAZY WATER

Family dinner is a special occasion at DeLaurenti. Not only does it provide a time to talk and learn about food, but it also allows one or more of the staff to cook something that means something to them. There is only one rule: the ingredients have to come from the store and/or the Market. With so much to choose from, it is no surprise that we eat well. Justin Lyon, former café manager turned personal chef, set the bar high with this recipe. He used to make it with his Calabrian grandfather. When Justin asked him what the secret was, he simply replied: "Just remember, the acqua pazza *is not thin like broth, or thick like sauce, the* acqua pazza *should be . . . splashy." It is perfect served individually or family style whenever you can get your hands on good spot prawns. Just be sure to have plenty of extra grilled bread on hand to mop up the broth.*

INGREDIENTS

4 large tomatoes

2 pounds spot prawns

⅓ cup plus 2 tablespoons extra-virgin olive oil, plus more
    for brushing and drizzling

6 garlic cloves, 5 thinly sliced and 1 left whole

1 onion, coarsely chopped

2 tablespoons tomato paste

1 cup dry white wine

2 cups water (approximately)

1 fennel bulb, shaved (white part only)

¼ cup capers

1 cup pitted Sicilian green olives, halved

1 teaspoon red pepper flakes

1 Macrina baguette

Salt

1 cup loosely packed chopped fresh Italian parsley,
    plus 1 big pinch for garnish

Juice of 1 lemon

Blanch the tomatoes in boiling water for 30 seconds, until the skins soften. Peel off the skins, then core, seed, and chop the tomatoes.

Shell the prawns, reserving the shells.

Heat ⅓ cup olive oil in a large saucepan over medium-low heat. Add 3 sliced garlic cloves, the onions and the prawn shells. Cook for 15 minutes, being careful not to burn the shells.

Turn the heat to medium, add the chopped tomatoes and tomato paste, and cook until the tomatoes release their juice. Add the wine, bring to a simmer, and cook until reduced by half, approximately 5 minutes. Add enough water to cover the shells and let simmer uncovered for 45 minutes.

Strain the broth, pushing on the shells and onions with a wooden spoon to extract all the liquid. Discard the shells. Set the broth aside. This can be made ahead and refrigerated for up to 2 days or frozen for up to a month.

When the broth is finished, add 2 tablespoons olive oil to a large saucepan. Add 2 sliced garlic cloves and cook over medium-low heat until just slightly colored. Add the fennel and cook until translucent, 8 to 10 minutes.

Add the capers, olives and red pepper flakes just to heat through. Add the reserved prawn stock to the pan and simmer over medium heat until reduced by a quarter.

While the stock reduces, slice the baguette, brush each piece with olive oil, and toast (or grill) until golden. Rub the bread slices with the last garlic clove.

Add the spot prawns to the "crazy water" and simmer for 1 to 2 minutes, or until just cooked through. Season the broth to taste with salt. Add the parsley and stir to blend.

To serve, place on a large warmed serving platter. Tuck the grilled bread, half in and half out, around the perimeter of the platter. Drizzle with extra-virgin olive oil and garnish with a healthy pinch of parsley. Finish with the lemon juice.

Serves 6

To drink: Pinot Bianco, Tavel, Bandol Rosé

BISTECCA ALLA FIORENTINA

If some people don't associate steak with Italian food, they haven't tried steak Florentine style. This dish marries three Tuscan staples: beef, olive oil and wine. Although tradition would require us to use meat from the region's Chianina breed of cattle, a good-quality T-bone or porterhouse from your favorite butcher will do, but it must be a T-bone or porterhouse. Similarly, nothing replicates the grassy, peppery quality of true Tuscan olive oil. As a general rule, the fewer ingredients you are using, the more they matter, and this matters. Finally, the wine: you won't find Chianti Classico or Brunello in the ingredients listed below, but without it, this recipe is not complete. *Although it is true that large cuts of meat typically seem more appropriate fare for cooler months, Bistecca alla Fiorentina is made for summer grilling. It is perfect served with a simple arugula salad and salsa verde on the side. Salsa verde is great with steak, but is equally delicious paired with pork, lamb, chicken or fish. If your meal needs a bit more substance, add a batch of Corona Beans with Olio Novello, Lemon and Italian Parsley (page 43).*

INGREDIENTS

4 1-inch-thick T-bone steaks

4 cups baby arugula

Best-quality Tuscan olive oil, for drizzling

Lemon wedges

Coarse sea salt

Freshly ground black pepper

Salsa Verde

1 bunch Italian parsley, leaves only

½ cup mint, leaves only, loosely packed

1 cup basil, leaves only, loosely packed

¼ cup capers, rinsed

1 garlic clove

3 anchovy fillets

1½ tablespoons lemon juice

1 cup extra-virgin olive oil

Salt and freshly ground pepper

Makes 1 cup

Remove the steaks from the refrigerator and let stand on the counter for 30 minutes.

Make the Salsa Verde: In a food processor, combine the parsley, mint, basil, capers, garlic, anchovies and lemon juice. Slowly add the olive oil and pulse until the sauce is smooth, but still has some texture. Season with salt and pepper to taste. This will keep in the refrigerator for up to a week.

Light a charcoal or gas grill.

Grill the steaks over high heat for about 4 to 5 minutes per side for medium-rare, or until done to your liking. Adjust the cooking time according to the thickness of the meat.

Transfer the steaks to a cutting board and let rest for 5 minutes.

Spread the arugula over a large serving platter and drizzle with a touch of olive oil, a squeeze of lemon and a pinch of sea salt. Carve the meat to your liking and serve on the bed of cold arugula.

Finish the steaks with a drizzle of olive oil, lemon wedges, and salt and pepper to taste. Serve salsa verde on the side.

Serves 4 to 6

To drink: Brunello di Montalcino, Chianti Classico

PIZZA *on the* BARBECUE

Making pizza is not normally thought of as a warm-weather activity; using your barbecue to do the cooking will change this perception. No special equipment is required; kettle and gas grills work equally well. Add a few apple or mesquite chips to the fire and you have a makeshift pizza oven. It's a fun process, it's easy, and it gets your kids and guests involved in doing some of the work! These pizzas are small and can be served as appetizers as well as a main course. The size is up to you, but in this case, smaller is better. They will be easier to handle on the grill, and you will have more options for toppings. As far as ingredients go, there are only two things to remember: simple and quality. There is no substitute for the best tomatoes, olive oil, cheese and cured meats. Whatever you choose, keep it simple, resist the temptation to be too heavy-handed, and use the best ingredients you can find.

INGREDIENTS

The Dough

2 teaspoons or 1 package active dry yeast
1½ cups warm water
1 teaspoon fine sea salt
1 tablespoon olive oil, plus more for oiling the bowl
4 cups Tipo 00 flour, high-gluten or all-purpose
Good-quality extra-virgin olive oil, for painting the crust

The Sauce

Red Sauce: 28-ounce can DOP San Marzano
 tomatoes, crushed by hand, or good-quality passata
White Sauce: 2 garlic cloves, minced, combined with
 ½ cup good-quality extra-virgin olive oil

In a large bowl, dissolve the yeast in the warm water and set aside until foamy, about 5 minutes. Add the salt, olive oil and half the flour. Using a wooden spoon, mix well to combine. Add the remainder of the flour little by little, incorporating it with your hands until you have formed a slightly sticky dough ball. You may have a bit of flour left over.

Transfer the dough to a lightly floured work surface and knead for 6 to 8 minutes, adding enough flour to form a dough that is smooth and elastic, but not sticky.

Form the dough into a ball and place in a lightly oiled bowl. Cover with a damp dish towel and let it rest for 90 minutes, or until it doubles in size.

Light a charcoal or gas fire.

Remove the dough from the bowl and divide into 4 equal pieces, fewer if you prefer larger pies. Dust a clean work surface with flour. Using a rolling pin or your hands, roll or push out the dough to ¼-inch thickness. Rustic is good—it's okay for them to not be perfectly round.

Grill the pizzas on one side only WITHOUT toppings for 1 to 2 minutes over a hot flame. Remove the pizzas to a board, flip them over, and spread the sauce and toppings on the CHARRED side of the crust. Paint the edge of the crust liberally with the extra-virgin olive oil.

Transfer back to the grill and finish cooking for 3 to 4 minutes, or until the toppings are done to your liking. Charred edges are good!

Toppings to Try

Cheeses: fresh mozzarella (well drained), Fontina Val d'Aosta, Parmigiano-Reggiano, Pecorino Romano, fresh chèvre, Mountain Gorgonzola, Asiago fresco, smoked mozzarella, truffle cheeses

Meats: prosciutto di Parma, Cascioppo's sausage, good-quality canned tuna, hot or sweet coppa, sopressata, artisan salame, braised meats

Vegetables: baby arugula, fresh spinach, grilled asparagus or eggplant, sautéed mushrooms, Italian parsley, grilled cherry tomatoes, roasted garlic, caramelized onions, broccoli rabe, heirloom tomatoes, sautéed kale

Other: capers, marinated olives, pine nuts, walnuts, fried egg, truffle oil, fresh herbs, truffle salt, pears

Makes 4 small pizzas

To drink: Aglianico, Nero d'Avola, Pinot Grigio, Rosé, Cold Beer

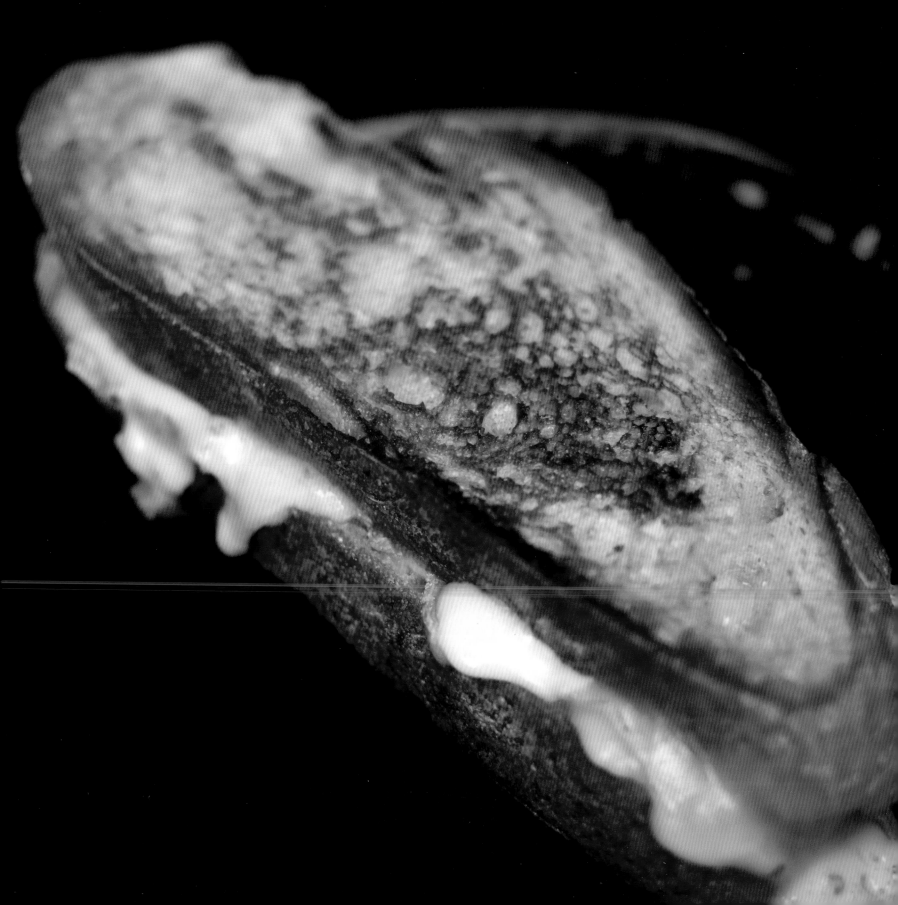

Whites

Riesling – Alsace, Austria, Germany, Oregon, Washington

Chardonnay – Burgundy, Italy, Oregon, Washington,
    anything unoaked

Sauvignon Blanc – Sancerre, Chile, Washington

Sparkling wine – Champagne, Prosecco, Cava

Northern Italy (Alto Adige, Friuli, Piedmont) – Pinot Grigio,
    Friulano, Arneis

Central Italy – Orvieto

Southern Italy – Greco di Tufo, Fiano

France (Loire Valley, Languedoc, Alsace) – Sancerre, Muscadet,
    Colombard, Pinot Blanc

Reds

Tuscany – Chianti, Sangiovese, Brunello

Piedmont – Barbera, Barolo, Barbaresco, Dolcetto

Southern Italy (Sardinia, Sicily, Puglia) – Frappato, Nero d'Avola,
    Primitivo, Aglianico

France – Languedoc, Bordeaux, Burgundy, Rhône, Cahors,
    Corbières, Morgon, Côtes-du-Rhône

Washington – Syncline Cellars, Cadence, Woodward Canyon,
    Andrew Will, Covington Cellars, Bunnell

Oregon – Pinot Noir

Spain – Garnacha, Rioja

Rosés

Provence, Bandol, Tavel, Oregon Pinot Noir

Champagne

Look for the RM on the label. It denotes "récoltant manipulant,"
which means the wine was produced by the grower of the grapes. This
is your symbol of true quality in Champagne. If it doesn't have the
RM, keep looking for one that does. Camille Savès and Jean Vesselle
Brut Réserve are fine choices.

SOUPS, SALADS & VEGETABLES

These recipes combine high-quality ingredients and simple preparations. Some you will find regularly on our café menu; others are favorites we love to make at home. Whether made at the shop or in our home kitchens, they all have one thing in common: the ingredients come from just inside or just outside our doors at DeLaurenti.

Easy recipes are even easier when you can get all your ingredients in one place. When these ingredients happen to be authentic Spanish chorizo, Yakima asparagus and Umbrian farro, the Pike Place Market is the place to go.

FAVA AL GUANCIALE

It seems like we have a lot of rules about eating: buy local; eat seasonal, fresh ingredients; simple is better; etc. And while these rules may appear to be a bit self-evident, it can be tough to assimilate them into our habits. Yet they make sense and require only a small amount of discipline. At no other time are these mantras truer than in July at the Pike Place Market. Fava beans emerge right after the rain stops on July 4th. Although shelling them can be somewhat time-consuming, it is absolutely worth the effort. The process is a lot faster when you enlist the help of family and friends, and it goes well with rosé and warm summer evenings. Although favas are fantastic on their own, the addition of a little pork fat really makes this dish come alive. You could use pancetta or bacon, but since DeLaurenti is at your disposal, take advantage of your ability to purchase cured pork jowl—guanciale. It has all the intense flavor of pork without the smoke, and pairs wonderfully with the beans. This is a great side dish or starter over crostini. Also, use this recipe as a platform for a grilled/sautéed salmon or halibut. Be sure to use the best olive oil you have.

INGREDIENTS

2 pounds whole fresh fava beans

3 ounces guanciale, ⅛-inch julienned (if you must substitute, pancetta will work)

3 tablespoons extra-virgin olive oil

¼ of a medium sweet onion, thinly slivered or finely chopped (Walla Walla sweet if available)

1 large garlic clove, thinly sliced

Salt and pepper

Remove the beans from the outer shells.

Prepare an ice bath by filling a large mixing bowl halfway with equal parts water and ice. Bring a medium saucepan of water to a boil. Blanch the beans in the boiling water for 2 minutes, then strain and transfer to the ice bath. When the beans are cool, drain and blot dry.

Remove the outer jackets of the beans. These steps will take a little time.

In a large skillet, sauté the guanciale in 1 tablespoon olive oil over medium heat until almost crispy, about 5 minutes. Remove the guanciale from the pan and set aside on paper towels. Remove excess fat and wipe the pan.

Add 1 tablespoon olive oil to the pan and heat until shimmering. Add the onions and garlic, and sauté for 3 minutes, until softened.

Add the fava beans and reserved guanciale. For larger beans, sauté 2 to 3 minutes. For smaller beans, simply heat through. Season to taste with salt and pepper. Garnish with the remaining 1 tablespoon olive oil.

Serves 4

To drink: Greco di Tufo, Pinot Bianco, Bright Chardonnay, Cannonau

ANCHO CHICKEN POZOLE

It's tough to find good pozole in Italy, but not at DeLaurenti. When our chef, Garrett Abel, makes this soup in our café, an alert goes out to our staff to reserve their bowl. This traditional Mexican stew proves that the Market is not just a good place for meats, fish and cheese, but it is also home to a wide array of dried peppers, hand-made tortillas and an endless supply of fresh garnish options. The ancho pepper, or dried poblano, has a deep, mildly smoky chile flavor without all the heat. In this recipe, the broth is the main event. We create a very intense puree that essentially turns the stock into a braising liquid. Making the puree takes a little bit of time, but it's well worth it. It is not only an irreplaceable ingredient in the soup, but it is also great to have around if you are making mole or pulled pork. Use chicken, pork, or both. Don't limit yourself to the minimum of garnishes; another bowl means another opportunity.

INGREDIENTS

2 pounds boneless, skinless chicken breast and/or pork shoulder, trimmed of extra fat and cut into 1-inch pieces

Salt and pepper

4 tablespoons olive oil

2 large yellow onions, cut in medium dice

4 garlic cloves, sliced thin

10 cups chicken stock

1½ cups Ancho Puree (see next page)

2 29-ounce cans white hominy, drained and rinsed well

Good-quality corn or flour tortillas

½ head of cabbage, shredded

Several radishes, sliced thin

1 bunch of cilantro, chopped

2 limes, cut into wedges

Season the meat liberally with salt and pepper. In a heavy-bottomed stockpot, heat the oil over high heat until it is almost smoking. Working in batches, brown the meat on all sides and transfer to a separate plate, 8 to 10 minutes total. Don't worry if it is not cooked all the way through.

Turn the heat down to medium and add the onions, garlic and a pinch of salt to the same pot. Sauté until softened and translucent, about 6 minutes. Add half of the stock and deglaze the pot, scraping up any browned bits. Add the ancho puree and simmer until there are no lumps. The liquid should be the consistency of a heavy stock base.

Return the meat and any juices to the stockpot and simmer gently, uncovered: 1 hour for chicken, 2 to 3 hours for pork (if using both, add the chicken halfway through the cooking process). The recipe can be made up to this point a day ahead and kept refrigerated.

Add the remaining stock and rinsed hominy and simmer for 30 minutes.

Using a pair of tongs, lightly char the tortillas over an open gas flame on the stove or grill on the barbecue.

Serve in warmed soup bowls and garnish with cabbage, shaved radishes, cilantro and a wedge of lime. Serve with the tortillas.

Note: Other garnish options are diced avocado, pickled red onions (see page 40), diced tomatoes, queso fresco and diced sweet onion.

Serves 8 to 10

To drink: Albariño, Oregon Pinot Gris, Your Favorite Beer

Ancho Puree

8 ounces ancho chiles
About 1 cup olive oil

In a saucepan, bring to a boil enough water to cover the chiles well. Place the chiles in the water and simmer for 5 minutes. Turn off the heat and let stand for 1 hour.

Pull the chiles from the water and remove the stems. Working in batches, puree the chiles in a food processor with just enough oil to emulsify, approximately 1 cup.

Pass the emulsified chile mixture through a food mill to remove the skin and seeds. Store, covered, in the fridge for a week or in the freezer for up to a month.

Makes approximately 4 cups

BLACK BEAN & CHORIZO SOUP

This is a DeLaurenti café favorite. Most of the time we make this soup with authentic Spanish chorizo; however, diced pork shoulder, bacon, ground beef or a combination of these also works well. A note of caution: don't add too much cayenne early in the process. With two hours of cooking time, it will get very hot. This soup is great made a day ahead, giving the flavors plenty of time to meld. Serve the garnishes on the side and accompany with charred tortillas and a cold beer.

INGREDIENTS

1 medium onion, diced

3 garlic cloves, chopped

6 tablespoons olive oil

2 15-ounce cans black beans, drained and rinsed

28-ounce can whole tomatoes, with juice, crushed by hand

1 tablespoon chili powder

1 teaspoon dried Mexican oregano

1 teaspoon cumin powder

¼ teaspoon cayenne pepper, more to taste

2 cups chicken stock

1½ pounds chorizo, diced

½ cup dry red wine

Salt and freshly ground pepper

Crème fraiche, chopped fresh cilantro, chopped scallions and lime wedges, for garnish

Best-quality tortillas, charred, for serving (see page 100)

In a heavy-bottomed soup kettle over medium heat, sauté the onions and garlic in 3 tablespoons olive oil until softened and translucent. Add the black beans, tomatoes, chili powder, oregano, cumin, cayenne and enough stock to cover.

In a sauté pan, heat 3 tablespoons olive oil until almost smoking. Add the chorizo and/or other meat and brown for 4 to 5 minutes. Add the wine and deglaze, scraping up any browned bits in the pan. Add the meat and liquid to the soup kettle. Season to taste with salt and pepper.

Simmer uncovered for 2 hours, adding more stock when necessary.

Garnish with crème fraiche, cilantro, scallions and lime wedges. Serve with charred tortillas.

Serves 8

To drink: Pilsner, Nero d'Avola

BLACK TRUFFLE POTATO LEEK SOUP

This soup was inspired by an encounter that our chef, Garrett Abel, had with potatoes poached in milk with black truffle. While he enjoyed eating them, he was thinking of what a great soup it would make. The next day, we served it in our café and it's been a fall favorite ever since. While the ingredients and cooking are quite simple, there are a few important steps to achieving the right texture.

INGREDIENTS

½ cup (1 stick) unsalted butter

1 pound leeks, white and pale green parts only, trimmed, split lengthwise, rinsed thoroughly and chopped into ¼-inch half-moons

½ large yellow onion, cut in medium dice

1 teaspoon chopped garlic

Kosher salt

2½ cups vegetable or chicken stock

2½ cups cream or milk

2 pounds Yukon Gold potatoes, peeled and cut in 1-inch dice

1 tablespoon good-quality black truffle oil, plus more to taste

Freshly ground pepper

Chives, finely diced, for garnish

Good-quality extra-virgin olive oil, for garnish

Fresh truffle, shaved for garnish (optional)

Crisp bacon bits, for garnish (optional)

First the food processor, and second the food mill. If you don't own a food mill, this is your opportunity to buy one. For this soup and many other sauces, it is the key to achieving a rich and silky texture. In this case, the finished product should be very smooth, but still have some body. You could attempt it with an immersion blender with some success, but be careful: too much blending will result in sticky soup.

Warm the butter in a large soup pot over medium-high heat. Add the leeks, onions, garlic and a pinch of salt and sauté until the onions are translucent and the leeks are wilted but not browned, about 6 to 7 minutes.

Meanwhile, combine the stock and cream and stir to blend.

Turn the heat down to medium. Add the potatoes to the soup pot and stir to coat with butter. Add enough of the stock/cream mixture to barely cover and bring to a gentle simmer. Add the truffle oil.

Simmer gently until the potatoes are completely tender. Remove from the heat and let cool for about 15 minutes. Working in batches, puree the soup in a food processor, then run the puree through a food mill into another pot. Repeat until all the soup is processed.

At this point, the mixture should have the consistency of runny mashed potatoes. Being conservative, whisk in the reserved stock/cream little by little until the soup is very smooth and silky, but still has some body. Put the soup back on low heat and bring to a bare simmer.

Add salt, pepper and more truffle oil to taste. Serve hot with a garnish of chives, a drizzle of olive oil and either truffle shavings or bacon bits.

Serves 6 to 8

To drink: Vermentino, Tavel or Rhone Rosé

FARRO SALAD *with* CHERRY TOMATOES, RED ONION, CUCUMBER *&* ARUGULA

This just might be the perfect dish. It's beautiful, delicious, healthy and easy to make. Like most good salads, it works well with variations. Try adding a little tuna or serve it alongside grilled steak or fish. Just be sure to use your best olive oil and enough salt and pepper. This salad also can be made a day ahead. For the best results on the second day, bring it to room temperature before serving and refresh it with a touch of olive oil and a squeeze of lemon.

INGREDIENTS

2 cups farro

2 tablespoons salt, plus more to taste

½ cup best-quality extra-virgin olive oil

1 tablespoon white wine vinegar

Juice of 1 lemon

Freshly ground black pepper

2 cups cherry tomatoes, halved

1 medium English cucumber, peeled and quartered, cut into bite-size pieces

¼ medium red onion, finely shaved

1 cup arugula, loosely packed

In a medium saucepan, combine the farro with 2 quarts water and 2 tablespoons salt. Bring to a boil over high heat. Reduce the heat to medium-low and simmer uncovered for 20 to 25 minutes, or until the farro is al dente. Rinse under cold water immediately, drain, and transfer to a large bowl.

Add 6 tablespoons olive oil, the vinegar, half of the lemon juice, and salt and pepper to taste. Stir to blend. Add the tomatoes, cucumbers, onions and arugula, and toss to coat. Finish with the remaining olive oil and lemon juice.

Serves 8 to 10 as a side dish

To drink: Dolcetto, Barbera or Soave

GRILLED ASPARAGUS *with* PEPERONCINI, PARMIGIANO-REGGIANO *&* LEMON ZEST

Few vegetables take to the grill as well as asparagus. When grilling any vegetable, the key is to use enough heat. This enables you to achieve the texture and flavor of a nice char without overcooking the *asparagus. This is delicious served alongside your favorite grilled meats or fish, at room temperature as part of an antipasto, or even chopped up and tossed with fresh pasta.*

INGREDIENTS

1 pound asparagus, cleaned

Extra-virgin olive oil

Kosher salt and freshly ground pepper

1 healthy pinch of red pepper flakes

Parmigiano-Reggiano, finely grated

Grated zest of ½ lemon

Light a barbecue, heat a grill pan on high, or preheat the oven to 450°F.

Snap the bottom off one piece of asparagus, noting where it breaks. Cut the rest of the bunch to the same length. Transfer to a roasting pan, lightly coat with olive oil, season liberally with salt and fresh pepper, and add the red pepper flakes.

If using a barbecue or grill pan, cook the spears directly over high heat, turning frequently, until they develop a nice char, but are still firm. If using the oven, roast the asparagus in the pan, shaking it occasionally to turn the spears until they develop the same nice char.

Remove from the heat and transfer to a platter. Dust with finely grated Parmigiano-Reggiano and garnish with lemon zest.

Serves 4

To drink: Gavi, Morellino di Scansano

GRILLED ROMAINE *with* CHARRED CHERRY TOMATOES, HAZELNUTS & SHAVED PECORINO

For obvious reasons, most people are reluctant to put fresh greens on a hot grill. To make this recipe work, you must be sure your grill is very hot. You want to develop a charred exterior without overcooking the romaine. When done, the greens should have a crispy texture on the outside with the inside barely warm. With the addition of crunchy toasted hazelnuts, grilled tomatoes and aged pecorino, this recipe can double as a light summer dinner with grilled bread.

INGREDIENTS

2 romaine lettuce hearts

½ cup hazelnuts

12 cherry tomatoes

8 tablespoons extra-virgin olive oil, plus more
    for coating tomatoes

Kosher salt and freshly ground pepper

2 tablespoons lemon juice

1 small shallot, minced

Aged pecorino, for shaving

Light a barbecue or heat a grill pan on medium-high.

Quarter the lettuce lengthwise, rinse and pat dry. Trim the stalks, leaving just enough to hold the leaves together.

In a small sauté pan over medium heat, toast the hazelnuts until fragrant but not burned. Let cool slightly, roughly chop, and set aside.

Coat the cherry tomatoes with olive oil and lightly salt and pepper. Set aside.

In a small bowl, combine the lemon juice, shallots, and salt and pepper to taste. Slowly whisk in the olive oil until emulsified.

Lay the romaine out on a sheet pan. Using a pastry brush, lightly brush the lettuce with some of the dressing and add a pinch of salt. Place the lettuce quarters, cut-side down, and tomatoes on the hot grill and cook until grill marks develop on both.

Transfer the romaine to 4 salad plates and divide the tomatoes equally. Drizzle each with the remaining dressing and top with toasted hazelnuts, shaved pecorino and fresh pepper.

Serves 4

To drink: Kerner

SPRING GREENS *with* CANDIED PECANS, DRIED CRANBERRIES, GOAT CHEESE *&* ORANGE

This is the DeLaurenti house salad—good enough to be on the menu of a nice restaurant but easy enough to have at home. Fresh and simple, it has a great juxtaposition of flavor and texture. Once you invest a small amount of time in preparing the ingredients, they can be used in a multitude of ways. The dressing is excellent with other salads and vegetables, while the pecans and dried cranberries are great companions for cheese. Honestly, most people choose this salad for the things we put on it. That being said, avoid the temptation to be heavy-handed on the accoutrements. Just enough is all you need.

INGREDIENTS

6 cups fresh wild greens

3 tablespoons Dijon Vinaigrette (see next page)

1 tablespoon dried cranberries

20 Candied Pecans (see below)

1 tablespoon crumbled goat cheese

8 orange segments (see next page)

Freshly ground pepper

In a large bowl, combine the greens with vinaigrette, tossing gently to coat.

Place the dressed greens on 4 chilled salad plates. Top with dried cranberries, pecans, goat cheese and orange segments. Add pepper to taste.

Serves 4

To drink: Arneis

Candied Pecans

These are easy to make and keep for a month in the cupboard. Making less than a pound is not a good use of your time.

1 sheet parchment paper

1 pound raw pecans

Grapeseed oil

¾ cup plus 2 tablespoons powdered sugar

Preheat the oven to 350°F. Line a baking sheet with parchment paper.

Bring a pot of water to a boil. Add the pecans and blanch for 1 minute.

Drain, transfer to a large mixing bowl, and add just enough oil to coat (too much oil and the nuts will not be crunchy). Working quickly, while they are still warm, add the sugar and stir until it dissolves and all the nuts are coated.

Transfer to the prepared baking sheet in a single layer and bake for 25 to 30 minutes, stirring and turning occasionally, until the nuts are evenly browned.

Let cool completely, then break the nuts apart and store in an airtight container.

Dijon Vinaigrette

⅓ cup Dijon mustard

2 tablespoons balsamic vinegar

1 tablespoon honey

2 tablespoons water

⅓ cup extra-virgin olive oil

Salt and pepper

Combine the mustard, vinegar, honey and water in a small mixing bowl. Slowly whisk in the olive oil until the dressing is smooth. Add salt and pepper to taste. Store in the refrigerator in an airtight container for 1 to 2 weeks. Bring to room temperature before using.

Makes a scant cup

Orange Segments

1 large seedless orange

Using a sharp knife, cut the ends off the orange just deep enough to expose the flesh. Place the orange cut-side down and cut away the peel in sections, following the orange's shape. Next, cut along the inside of the membranes that separate the orange segments, slicing only down to the center of the orange. Continue around the entire orange, removing each segment as you go and placing them in a bowl. Squeeze the juice from the remaining membrane into the bowl with the segments. Store the oranges in their own juice, covered and refrigerated.

DESSERTS

The shelves at DeLaurenti are full of an amazing selection of chocolate, cookies and confections, but we are especially proud of the desserts that come from our own kitchen. At 11 a.m. warm cookies and brownies parade down the stairs and into the café, and most Thursdays, a fresh Torta di Mandorle with seasonal fruit is on the table for our staff meetings. These recipes are special to us because of their connection to our store—to the staff whose input helped create them and to the customers who come every day to enjoy them.

TORTA DI MANDORLE

Our management team meets every Thursday at 7 a.m. We generally discuss the goings-on in the store relative to the various departments to make sure we're on the same page for the week. While we would like to believe that our wonderful managers eagerly look forward to this invigorating exchange of ideas and commentary, I know the real reason they show up two hours before the store opens is Connie's (our deli buyer) Torta di Mandorle. Connie doesn't make it every week— she mixes it up every now and then—but the memorable meetings are those when a torta is involved. She'll put whatever local fresh fruit is in season into the mix, and it's usually a surprise. In the winter, the torta is served straight-up. For variety, we'll whip up a berry conserve (recipe below). As we finish our meeting, we know we are armed with good info about the store and sustenance from our most important team member: the Torta di Mandorle. While we enjoy this in the morning, it's completely at home for dessert. Simple to make and rewarding, it can be prepared up to a day in advance.

INGREDIENTS

½ cup fine cornmeal

½ cup cake flour

1 teaspoon baking powder

½ cup (1 stick) unsalted butter, at room temperature

¼ cup almond paste, diced

1¼ cups powdered sugar, plus more for dusting

½ teaspoon vanilla extract

2 large eggs

4 large egg yolks

¼ cup sour cream (or crème fraiche)

Preheat the oven to 350°F. Grease a 9-inch round cake pan with butter and dust with flour.

In a bowl, combine the cornmeal, cake flour and baking powder. Mix well and set aside.

With a mixer using the paddle attachment, beat the butter and almond paste on high until smooth, about 3 to 5 minutes. Reduce the speed to low and slowly add the powdered sugar. Mix until combined and airy.

Raise the speed to high. Add the vanilla and then the whole eggs and egg yolks, one at a time. Mix until well combined. The batter may look "sticky" or separated. Reduce the speed to medium and add the sour cream and dry ingredients. Mix until just incorporated.

Pour the batter into the prepared cake pan and smooth the surface with a spatula. Bake in the *lower third* of the oven for 30 to 35 minutes, or until a toothpick inserted in the center comes out clean. Transfer the pan to a wire rack and let cool. When cool, remove the cake from the pan and dust with powdered sugar.

Serves 8 to 12

To drink: Vin Santo, Beaumes de Venise

Berry Conserve Garnish

1 cup frozen or fresh seasonal berries
2 tablespoons powdered sugar

In a saucepan, combine the berries and sugar. Cook over medium heat, mashing the berries and stirring frequently until the sauce thickens to a syrup consistency. Drizzle over the cake slices and serve.

Makes about 1 cup

CHOCOLATE CHIP COOKIES

For all the great food there is to enjoy in the world, there are few things better than a perfect chocolate chip cookie fresh from the oven. Reaching consensus on this recipe required us to eat a lot of cookies— no easy task. We each entered into the process with our own biases: the edges had to have a bit of a caramelized crunch, the middle had to be gooey but not doughy, and the quality of the chocolate had to be evident. We must have done something right, because the end result earned us Best in Show honors in Seattle *magazine's Best Desserts*

issue. A few tips: The resting period for these cookies is important. It gives the flour and the egg time to bond, which results in better texture and flavor. Without it, they can turn out a bit cakey. Additionally, if the tops of your cookies turn out perfectly but the bottoms always burn, a small investment in a good sheet pan will fix it. So plan ahead and double the recipe. The dough holds for a week in the fridge or up to a month in the freezer. If this is all too much, just come down to DeLaurenti at 11 a.m. The cookies will still be warm.

INGREDIENTS

1 cup (2 sticks) unsalted butter, at room temperature

1 cup firmly packed dark brown sugar

1 cup granulated sugar

2 large eggs

1½ teaspoons vanilla extract

1 teaspoon fine sea salt

1 teaspoon baking soda

3 cups all-purpose flour

2 cups Callebaut bittersweet chocolate chips

Parchment paper

Set up the mixer with the paddle attachment. On low speed, cream together the butter and sugars for approximately 1 minute or until light and fluffy.

Add the eggs one at a time, waiting until the first egg is fully incorporated before adding the second. Mix in the vanilla, sea salt and baking soda.

Add the flour 1 cup at a time until just incorporated. Add the chocolate chips and mix until they are evenly distributed. Remove the dough from the mixing bowl, wrap in plastic, and transfer to the refrigerator.

ALLOW THE DOUGH TO REST, REFRIGERATED, FOR 24 HOURS.

After the resting period, adjust the oven racks to the upper and lower middle positions, and preheat the oven to 350°F. Line 2 cookie sheets with parchment paper.

Portion the dough into 2-ounce balls, about the size of a golf ball. Tear the dough balls in half, join them back together by the bottom/sides (see photo), place on the prepared cookie sheets 3 inches apart, and lightly press down. This will give you a nice rustic top.

Bake for 12 to 15 minutes, or until the edges are golden brown and the center is light and puffy. For evenly baked cookies, halfway through the cooking time, switch the cookie sheet positions from upper to lower racks and front to back. Transfer the cookies to a rack to cool for 5 to 10 minutes. Enjoy warm.

Yields approximately 21 2-ounce cookies

BITTERSWEET BROWNIES

There are two different types of people in the kitchen, the cooks and the bakers. Rarely can people do both. Our former chef Meghan Boyle was one of the few who could. She had the ability to hear our requests and make the translation. At the store, we all could agree on two things: 1. Brownies could be found everywhere. 2. None of us wanted to eat the ones we found. We set out to change this. Ours had to be the right texture: not too cakey, not too gooey. They had to have a paper-thin sugary sheen. The edges had to be crusty. And last, they had to taste like really good chocolate. We think we achieved what we *set out to do. Apart from the process itself, the two most important components of this recipe are the chocolate and the vanilla. Of the many chocolates we have at our disposal, we found that Callebaut bittersweet gave us the best results. Likewise, there is no substitute for pure Tahitian vanilla. Its intense, fruity, sweet aroma has no equal. If you have ever wondered why these brownies are so good, this is the reason.*

INGREDIENTS

4 large eggs

2 teaspoons Tahitian vanilla

1 cup firmly packed dark brown sugar

1 cup granulated sugar

1 cup (2 sticks) butter

8 ounces Callebaut bittersweet chocolate

½ teaspoon sea salt

1 cup sifted all-purpose flour

Preheat the oven to 325°F. Butter a 9-by-13-inch baking pan.

In a medium bowl, thoroughly whisk together the eggs, vanilla and sugars until frothy and lump-free. Set aside.

Using a double boiler or a glass bowl set over a pan of boiling water, melt together the butter, chocolate and sea salt. Stir well. Add the chocolate mixture to the egg mixture and blend thoroughly.

Add the sifted flour to the chocolate and eggs. Mix together gently. Do not overmix. Pour the batter into the buttered pan. Bake for 25 minutes.

To test, insert a wooden skewer into the center of the brownies. When the skewer comes out clean, the brownies are done. Let the brownies cool in the pan for 30 minutes. Then cut to the desired size.

Yields approximately 8 to 12 brownies

TRADITIONAL BISCOTTI

We used to do a monthly wine club and we included a recipe with each month's wines. Vin Santo was featured one month and a biscotti recipe was a natural addition. As you can gather by now, a traditional and simple recipe was in order. As a good son, Pat enrolled *his father in the club and he took this recipe—very similar to his Italian mother's, which wasn't written down—and perfected it. Mr. McCarthy is a retired engineer, so be assured that it has been tested hundreds of times and is perfectly accurate in every detail.*

INGREDIENTS

1 cup blanched whole almonds

½ cup (1 stick) unsalted butter, melted

2 cups granulated sugar

1½ tablespoons vanilla extract, or 1½ tablespoons anise extract or flavoring

5 large eggs

5 cups all-purpose flour

3 tablespoons baking powder

½ teaspoon salt

A few things to consider with this recipe:

1. Blanched almonds are hard to find (find them at DeLaurenti). Do not substitute any other almond; it just won't taste right.

2. This makes a medium-hard cookie. If you want them harder, use fewer eggs. Softer, use more eggs.

3. This is a sticky dough. Keep your hands well-floured.

4. Have a 6-inch dough scraper on hand.

Preheat the oven to 400°F.

Spread the almonds in one layer on a cookie/baking sheet. Toast until golden, 6 to 10 minutes.

Turn the oven down to 350°F.

In a mixer, combine the melted butter, sugar and vanilla, then mix. Add the eggs and mix well.

Add the flour, baking powder and salt. Mix well and then add the toasted almonds. The dough will be pliable but on the runny side.

On a hard surface dusted with flour, divide the dough into 4 equal portions. Form the dough balls into oblong loaves about 6 inches in length and transfer to 2 cookie sheets (2 per sheet).

Bake the loaves for 40 minutes and remove from the oven. Let cool for 2 minutes. While the loaves are still warm, slice them crosswise into individual, equal pieces about ¾ inch thick. Place the pieces on a cookie sheet and toast until just golden, about 10 minutes. Turn the pieces over and bake for another 8 to 10 minutes, until golden.

Yields approximately 32 biscotti

Wine: Vin Santo

INDEX